ROSWELL

THE AFTER-ACTION REPORT

GREG LAWSON, M.ED.

BEYOND THE FRAY

Publishing

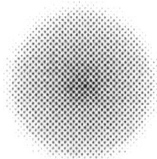

BEYOND THE FRAY

Publishing

For Lynn – you were correct – mostly...

"Men stumble over the truth from time to time, but most pick themselves up and hurry off as if nothing happened."

Winston Churchill

CONTENTS

You are about to take a journey on what has been considered well-trod territory, a story you think you know inside and out, but this book takes an interesting twist with the examination of all facets of these accounts by a man with honorable military credentials, an extensive law enforcement background, and unique investigative techniques to dig through the red tape of military interference, previous inept investigations, and carefully crafted "final words" by our government and armchair detectives alike.

Author Greg Lawson is a man whose integrity I respect, whose passion for uncovering the truth is unparalleled. He is a man who is willing to make the tough calls on previous eyewitness testimony, from both the believers and nonbelievers alike, from respected military insiders to Roswell residents, in an effort to shake the paradigm we have been willing to ascribe to, far too long and willingly.

Few stories in the American experience have captured the imagination and fascination as much as the reported crash of a "flying saucer" in Roswell, New Mexico, in 1947. Although many things have been said about this case, from first military responders to locals, there is much speculation as to what exactly unfolded in that sleepy little town, a town that is forever trapped in time on that Tuesday, July 8 of 1947.

Uncovering the truth can come at a price, but we are at a new crossroads in American history, a place where our government seems to be willingly participating in a slow, steady form of disclosure of some sort regarding unidentified aerial phenomena. The price of breaking the truth while exposing the lies, disinformation and misdirection of the past is probably at the lowest cost it will ever be. With the majority of the main principals involved in this historically significant moment in time having passed away, the demand for the truth is at an all-time high, and the eyes of the world are turned toward us now more than ever to lead the way in sharing the truth, the whole truth, and nothing but the truth.

Whether you are a believer in visitors from outer space, interdimensional travelers or covert military experimental flying machines, this book considers every aspect and theory in the hopes of uncovering the logic in what at times may appear to be illogical situations. We deserve the truth and an understanding as to why the government that is here to protect us and watch out for our best interests seems to have undeniably hidden things from us when it comes to our place in the ever-expanding universe.

The one fact we do know is that something big happened that day, an event that shaped how we moved forward in reporting and investigating UFO phenomena. Were there bodies of otherworldly beings recovered? Did our massive leaps in technology really spring from what was recovered from the wreckage or merely inspired by the science fiction claims surrounding the reported incident? Are we being visited by superior beings with technology that far surpasses our own, or are we the masters of deception, misdirection and playing the ultimate game of smoke and mirrors, not just with American citizens but the citizens of the world?

As the host of the long running paranormal-themed podcast and radio program *Darkness Radio*, I personally have spoken to people from every walk of life regarding the Roswell crash. Dr. Jesse Marcel Jr. told me that he believed the US government was deceiving the world and that he was witness to one of the greatest cover-ups in history. Dr. Marcel and his father served long distinguished careers in the military despite their claims, which leads me to believe that if they were insane, liars or had an illicit agenda, they would not have continued to be held in high regard and called back into active duty to serve their country. These men, along with many others, saw things firsthand, things that they swore were real and not of this world. Are they part of the bigger game to keep us guessing or patriots who stood for the truth and fact? I have dug deeply into this case for over fifteen years in hopes of getting a full understanding of the story, but something always seemed to be eluding me, until this book.

Open your mind and prepare to be enlightened for perhaps the first time in a comprehensive look into this case in a way that has never been examined as uniquely and objectively as this. This book is not about exaggerating the facts or hiding them, it is about revealing them for what they are, as they should have been from the start, and come what may, you are guaranteed to never think of this case the same way again.

Onward and upward, my friends. Enjoy.

PREFACE

In June of 1947, the stage was set for one of the biggest governmental cover-ups in American history. The state of New Mexico was considered out of the way and was sparsely populated. It was an ideal area for secret military projects and for testing nuclear weapons. Between aerial activities at the Roswell Army Airfield and the experimental craft coming from the testing grounds at Alamogordo, the area was rife with tales of strange objects in the sky and reported UFOs as well.

It is difficult to decipher the Roswell "code." Most of the distraction and complexity of explanations provided by the US government was designed to intentionally compound confusion of the event. The investigation was additionally exacerbated by what we know now as intentional hoaxers—uninvolved people who want to become part of the story or are simply entertained by watching investigators head down the wrong path. Their motivations can vary from the desire to attain fame, to monetary gain, or to just have fun watching the proverbial train wreck. This is a well-known phenomenon in law enforcement investigations. In one particular case in Austin, Texas, four teenage girls were murdered at a local yogurt shop, and the building was intentionally burned. Initially, investigators did not realize there was anyone inside the building until they found the gruesome remains. During the subsequent investigation, forty-two people came forward to admit they had committed the murders. Forty-two people wanted to be known for murdering four high-school-aged girls. For normal people, such a thing is unthinkable. However, each one of the confessors were slowly eliminated from the suspect pool due to their inaccurate knowledge of the crime scene and other circumstances that proved it was impossible for them to be at that location at the time. Hundreds of investigative man-hours wasted chasing false trails.

To this day, the yogurt shop case has never been solved.

The real puzzle to an investigation in which self-confessing witnesses come forward with erroneous information is determining at what point do you start believing the suspect's testimony and at what point do you draw the line at their deception?

The events that happened in June and July of 1947, now referred to as the "Roswell Incident," provides a unique challenge to anyone who is a professional investigator and is and remains objective to the evidence provided. That objectivity has to be evaluated. Investigators must consider the absence of physical evidence, insufficiency of forensic or latent evidence, the lack of documentary evidence available and compare this to the abundant circumstantial and testimonial evidence collected by some of the most dedicated citizen investigators in the world. The amount of time, travel, and expenses incurred by men like Don Schmidt and Tom Carey is unbelievable. According to these two particular men, they have interviewed over seven hundred people. While many of the interviews gleaned no new or substantial information, and much of the information would be considered hearsay in a criminal court, the sheer volume of these professed witnesses does add weight to their validity. And there are many other investigators over the last forty years who have helped to shed the light on this very confusing case.

Hence, professional investigators must not only have the

ability to collect physical evidence, and the skill to obtain testimonial evidence, they must also be skeptical of both. They must be willing to go beyond the obvious and test the unknown. They must be willing to turn over evidence recovered for examination as well as qualifying the individual witnesses who espouse to being involved. In the pursuit of the truth, it is as important to identify exculpatory evidence and deceptions as it is to relate items and situations to the incident.

Whenever a person conducts an investigation, there are certain things you should look for. The evidence used to build a case comes in the forms of physical, testimonial, circumstantial, demonstrative, documentary, forensic, latent, statistical, and exculpatory. Testimonial and circumstantial are often the most controversial types. And it is the testimonial evidence that is often categorized as anecdotal, character, and hearsay and often found biased and inaccurate. This is why investigators look to qualify their witnesses. They looked to put a stamp of approval on the information they receive. That is why when scientists or law enforcement personnel come forward to relate a fantastic story, it becomes even more intriguing. In the case of Roswell, hundreds, maybe over a thousand people have been interviewed by various Roswell investigators. Most of these citizen researchers have never worked as a paid, professional investigator—they are mostly hobbyists, journalist, and freelance writers. I am not saying the average person cannot conduct an investigation, what I am saying is without protocols and methods that guide your inquiries, you're just flying by the seat of your pants.

More importantly, in this case you must also understand this incident was buried for thirty-one years. From the time it was initially reported in the *Roswell Daily Record* to the time it was recanted and buried was less than forty-eight hours. While several newspaper articles were written throughout the United States, the story was quickly quashed. And it wasn't until 1978 that Stanton Freeman, a nuclear physicist and amateur ufolo-gist, was told by a Baton Rouge radio manager of the Roswell flying saucer story. In addition, the manager provided Friedman with the pivotal military eyewitness to the crash debris, Jesse Marcel. If it had not been for Marcel's testimony, this incident may have remained in obscurity.

When conducting an inquiry into a case such as Roswell, the investigator must understand that they are dealing with a cold case. They must understand the context of the information they gather and not evaluate it with their contemporary stan-dards. They must have a good understanding of the social and cultural environments in which the information was obtained and in which the incident occurred.

In the case of the Roswell Incident, the military parties involved were in a transitional state. What I mean is, two months after the debris was recovered, on September 18, 1947, the United States Army Air Forces transformed and became the United States Air Force. This had been a slow and methodical process intended to consolidate the Air Force and provide a clearer mission for the organization. This was a time of flux and reorganization. New policies and procedures. New mission statements. A new chain of command.

Truly a new beginning.

It was in late June and early July 1947, two months before this historic transition, the most celebrated, investigated, and controversial UFO report surfaced, commonly known as the "Roswell Incident."

ACKNOWLEDGMENTS

For over a decade, I have interviewed dozens of relevant and knowledgeable persons about Roswell. I have attended numerous conferences and far too many lectures. I have collected and compiled the works of many Roswell investigators, researchers, bloggers, and writers. These piles of papers and stacks of books have sat idly on my desk for years, waiting for something to spur my enthusiasm and move me to the next step, actually writing a book. As the years passed, many people asked if I had completed the book. Then they asked if I was close to finishing the book. Then finally they asked if I had even started the book. Well, I can say definitively, the book is now finished. I would like to thank so many people in the UFO and paranormal community for their support and encouragement to complete what is and will be a very controversial topic.

Outside of my wife Lynn's consistent support, there has been one person who has always encouraged me and kept me involved in the mix when it comes to Roswell, and that is TV personality and radio host Dave Schrader. If it were not for Dave Schrader's encouragement, influence, and guest appearances on *Darkness Radio*, *Beyond the Darkness*, *Midnight in the Desert*, and *Coast to Coast*, I most likely would still be languishing in a sea of muddled facts, disturbing testimonies, and questionable documents. Thank you, Dave, for your influence, guidance, and friendship.

I would also like to thank:

Brad Blair of the Michigan Paracon and *The Creaking Door Podcast*. Years ago, Lynn and I traveled to Romania to follow the trail of Dracula through Transylvania with Dave Schrader. In the process we met Brad Blair and have maintained a great friendship ever since. Brad too has encouraged my Roswell project and further allowed me to be a part of the annual paracon in Sault Ste Marie. This has given me great exposure and provided a foundation for my success in the paranormal community—something I truly appreciate.

Tom Carey and Don Schmitt for their tireless efforts to unmask the Roswell story and the many good conversations both on the phone and in Roswell itself. And specifically for Tom for taking me into his confidence and allowing me to briefly be a part of the work. I wish I could have been more fruitful. You both inspired me to dig deeper and to think.

And finally, thanks to all the believers and debunkers who are professional enough to come together to discuss, debate, argue, and go forth again in search of the truth. We need more productive discourse and less petty bickering.

INTRODUCTION

It was sometime in 1989 or 1990 when I watched an *Unsolved Mysteries* program about Roswell. I was extremely surprised and intrigued by the possibility that in 1947 an alien spacecraft may have crash-landed in the high desert of New Mexico. What did not surprise me was the fact that the United States military covered it up. That was all it took; I was hooked on watching the skies.

In the early 1980s, at the height of the Cold War, I served as a paratrooper with the United States Army. International deceit and deception were the rules of the day. Any substantial military operation, including training, had some form of counterintelligence plan included—some convoluted story to divert the attention of the curious toward another direction. I spent two of those years in Alaska, studying Soviet tactics and waiting for a possible Soviet military operation to cross the Bearing Sea and reclaim Alaska for the Russians. Back then there was always a Boeing E-3 Sentry, Airborne Early Warning and Control (AWACS) aircraft in the sky with fighter escort as they did daily intercepts of Russian aircraft over the North Pacific and Bering Sea. It was there I saw a couple of additional UFOs. Unfortunately, it didn't take me long to realize they were manmade satellites. But in 1984, there were very few visible satellites. Today with an easily available app, you can see several satellites in an hour. When I left Alaska in 1984, the environment remained tense at Fort Richardson as well as Elmendorf Air Force Base, dealing with the Soviet threat.

Once I separated from the Army, I began my law enforcement career as a deputy sheriff. During my tenure I have worked patrol, as a mental health investigator, suicide mediator, hostage negotiator, SWAT team member, scuba team leader, academy instructor, child abuse and sex crimes detective, homicide detective, as a lake patrol and underwater recovery team sergeant, and as a patrol lieutenant. Along the way I earned a master's degree in education with an academic concentration in Complex Adaptive Systems (CAS) and Complex Adaptive Human Systems (CAHS), a fancy way of explaining how to manage and predict change in large organizations. However, while this is a helpful analytical tool, psychologists have not yet perfected predicting human behavior.

Predicting human behavior is possibly the most challenging part of a criminal investigation. While the world has gotten wrapped around the proverbial forensic axel, with shows such as *Dexter*, *Bones*, and any of the *CSI* "Insert City Here" shows, hobbyist sleuths routinely imagine solving a murder by working through the evidence in forty-three minutes. Just like on TV. While collecting evidence is a vital role in establishing motive, intent, and circumstances, I have learned that the interviewing of witnesses, victims, suspects, and other involved persons is often the key to a non-TV or real-world investigation. While evidence such as cell phone data is important, real-world cases are usually solved through the people involved, their actions, and their testimony.

Never give up the opportunity to listen.

As a major crimes detective, I have worked or assisted in cases where I knew exactly who committed the murder. You would think case solved, right? But that is far from the truth. You may know, due to certain circumstances, coincidences, and good instinct that one particular individual killed another. Sometimes this information is gathered from apparent subtle body language during an interview, a glance of the eye, or unnatural body gestures, too much eye contact, not enough eye contact, etc. But those by themselves are not the foundation of forming a criminal indictment. These things must be supported by other forms of evidence.

I have personally witnessed law enforcement officers and detectives establish a preconceived notion of an individual's culpability in a crime—even before they begin investigating the crime. Ideas just based off of the original report and the first meeting with the suspect. I refer to these instincts being based off of the investigator's own values, assumptions, beliefs, and expectations (VABEs). These are more often than not influencers of the case disposition and are completely separate of the physical evidence of the event. In some of these cases, the law enforcement professional was correct.

But in some of these cases they were not.

During my career in law enforcement, I took two breaks. One I served four years as an operations specialist in the United States Navy on board USS *Nimitz* from 1990 to 1994. The other was a period in the US Air Force security forces in 1997 and 1998—looking back, I didn't think I would ever live this long... But this variety of experience and my education provides me with a unique perspective on possibilities.

In the following pages of this book, I will explain and examine the key players of the Roswell Incident. I will recount their stories, examine their assertions, and identify their deceptions. This will include the witnesses, the suspects, and the investigators as well. I will not complicate these observations with arguments of exactly what time, what day, I am not concerned with whether or not a person involved normally went by their nickname instead of their given name, I will not be bogged down by the typical minutiae that many Roswell supporters or detractors become quagmired in. This is not a case file being brought to the grand jury for indictment. It is not a deposition of fact to be scrutinized for a technicality. It is a series of observations designed to help us move forward and, hopefully, not make the same mistakes next time. It is a discussion of the lessons learned from the Roswell affair. This is a journey that will bring us that much closer to the truth.

And some can't handle the truth...

COMING CLEAN WITH BRIGADIER GENERAL THOMAS DUBOSE

FORMER COLONEL AT FORT WORTH ARMY AIRFIELD 1947

Brigadier General Thomas Dubose

AS FAR AS THE NUMBER ONE EYEWITNESS TO THE COVER-UP of the conspiracy to deceive the American people, the designation of "whistleblower" would have to go to then Colonel Thomas DuBose. Roswell investigators and the skeptics as well do not debate the fact that the initial Roswell Incident as portrayed to the public was a hoax. It was a cover story to frame much more complex circumstances. Some believe it was to cover the evidence of a secret balloon project, and some believe it was to cover up an extraterrestrial encounter. Some would think that Major Jesse Marcel has the whistleblower distinction; however, Marcel was not privy to the planning phase or part of the organizational team that carried out the deception —DuBose was.

It is here the debate begins...

I am coming at the Roswell Incident with nearly thirty years as a career cop and professional criminal investigator. The investigative approach employed by a state or local law enforcement official is different from a federal approach. It is certainly different from a military, CIA, NSA, FBI or any other three-letter-acronym approach method you choose. At the state and local level, we do not have unlimited resources. We do not have teams of agents working on the same case. We certainly do not have months of time to conclude a thousand-page report of what is usually mostly fluff, conjecture, and useless information from persons whose testimony does not pertain to circumstances proving the offense or incident was committed by an identified perpetrator. In other words, during my investigations, I cannot afford to get off the trail and lost in the weeds. With that said, I will not be reviewing this case in a chronological manner—I will be reviewing it in a contextual manner relative to the importance of the information provided—in my opinion.

As a property crimes detective (burglary, theft, criminal mischief, etc.), I was not assigned a case and then worked it from beginning to end, then get assigned another case and worked it from beginning to the end—that's television. I was assigned several cases on Monday, several on Tuesday, several on Wednesday, etc. At certain times of the year, I might have had fifty active cases, all of which I was juggling and trying to keep the facts and circumstances straight. As a persons crimes detective (assault, stalking, harassment, etc.), I was assigned about half the caseload of the property crimes detectives. And as a major crimes detective (homicide, sexual assault, robbery, etc.), I was assigned plus or minus fifteen a month. The main challenge in each discipline is managing your caseload. You have to know when to move forward, when to get a warrant, and when to give up.

Within these pages, I have attempted to boil down the Roswell Incident to the point of what matters. What are the circumstances within the case that indicate it is something more than it appears on the surface? What is the totality of the circumstances that would lead a reasonable person to believe the events were as the Air Force describes in their official report *The Roswell Report – Fact vs. Fiction in the New Mexico Desert*, or was it something more along the way the Roswell civilian investigative community portrays them?

To start, let's see if we can at least all agree on certain aspects of the investigation using information that was recorded at the time of the events and from the testimony of those actually involved firsthand.

I think we can all relatively agree that according to various documentation at the time, somewhere between June 14, 1947, and July 7, 1947, several events occurred in New Mexico that led up to suspicious circumstances relating to the Roswell Army Airfield. There could be many more considerations; however, I have boiled them down to the following points of review.

1. On July 2, 1947, at ~approximately 10 p.m., Roswell citizen **Dan Wilmot (possible circumstantial witness)** reported seeing a glowing object travelling northwesterly at a high rate of speed. He reports this to the *Roswell Daily Record* just before the July 8, 1947, printing of the capture of a flying saucer.

2. **William Ware (Mack) Brazel (eyewitness)**

finds some strange material on the Foster Ranch, about seventy-five miles northwest of Roswell.

3. Brazel notifies his neighbors **Floyd and Loretta Proctor (witnesses)** and shows them some of his findings. They encourage him to report it to the authorities.

4. On or about Sunday, July 6, 1947, Brazel brought some of the material he had found to Chaves County **Sheriff George Wilcox (witness)** in Roswell.

5. Wilcox in turn notifies the Roswell Army Airfield and relays the information.

6. Intelligence officer **Major Jesse Marcel (eyewitness / conspirator / whistleblower)**, and military counterintelligence personnel **Captain Sheridan Cavitt (eyewitness / conspirator)**, and per some accounts **Master Sergeant Bill Rickett (eyewitness / conspirator)** accompanied Brazel back to the ranch.

7. The men collected an unspecified amount of suspicious shiny material from the site described by Marcel in a videoed interview as three-quarters of a mile long and several hundred feet wide.

8. Cavitt and possibly Rickett are reported to fill a military vehicle with debris and returned to the RAAF.

9. Major Marcel collected additional debris in his car and stopped by his residence on his way back to the RAAF and showed it to his wife and son, **Jesse Marcel Jr. (witness).**

10. According to a later official RAAF written statement, the material was reviewed by RAAF

personnel and determined to possibly be one of the recent media-reported flying disks.

11. The RAAF commander **Col. William Blanchard (witness / conspirator)** approves a press release through public information officer (PIO) **Lt. Walter Haut (conspirator)**, admitting the same and claiming to have a flying disc in their possession.

12. The *Roswell Daily Record* changes the wording of the official RAAF press release from "disc" to "saucer" and from "gain possession" to "captures," then publishes the front-page article as: "RAAF Captures Flying Saucer on Ranch in Roswell Region." Very catchy…

13. **General Roger Ramey (perpetrator / conspirator)** of Fort Worth Army Airfield's Eighth Air Force orders Marcel to fly the material to him in Texas.

14. Marcel does so and participates in photos at General Ramey's office, as does **Colonel Thomas DuBose (conspirator / witness)**, **Warrant Officer Irving Newton (witness)**, and *Fort Worth Star-Telegram* photographer **J. Bond Johnson (witness)** with what is common weather balloon material.

15. On July 9, 1947, an additional press statement is released recanting the flying saucer story and replacing it with the new weather balloon story.

16. Inquiries, research, and further direct documentation essentially disappears for thirty-one years until **Stanton Friedman's (ufologist / theorist)** meeting with Major Jesse Marcel in 1978.

17. The investigation of the Roswell Incident is reopened by part-time, yet very dedicated and intelligent ufologists.

18. The Governmental Accounting Office opens up an official inquiry into the incident in 1994 at the request of **Congressman Steven H. Schiff (elected official enquirer)** of New Mexico.

19. In 1995 the Air Force releases *The Roswell Report – Fact vs. Fiction in the New Mexico Desert* authored by USAF **Colonel Richard L. Weaver (USAF investigator / debunker)** and **Lieutenant James McAndrew (USAF investigator / debunker)**. The report determined the crash debris recovered on the Foster Ranch was that of a 1947 top-secret surveillance balloon project named MOGUL, with the intent to spy of the Soviet government.

20. Investigators such as **Stanton Friedman (ufologist), Kevin Randle (ufologist), Don Schmitt (ufologist), Tomas Carey (ufologist)**, and many others not listed here continue to accuse the government agencies involved in the final Air Force reports of continuing to cover up elements of the event.

21. In 1997, the Air Force releases an additional report titled *The Roswell Report – Case Closed*, authored by **USAF Captain James McAndrew (USAF investigator / debunker)**. The report is an attempt to clarify the USAF's position on MOGUL and that witnesses did not see aliens at various locations. The Air Force conclusion is that anthropomorphic parachute test dummies used by the Air Force during projects High Dive and

Excelsior were misidentified as aliens by citizens who came across them in a variety of ways. Although High Dive and Excelsior started roughly six years after the Roswell Incident, Air Force officials equated this to long-term memory distortions, false memories, and psychological time compression of other unrelated events. They relied so much on these distortions it reminded me of *A Christmas Carol* by Charles Dickens:

"You may be an undigested bit of beef, a blot of mustard, a crumb of cheese, a fragment of an underdone potato. There's more gravy than grave about you, whatever you are."

The charges leveled by ufologists are based on the government's (1) lack of documentation of the event, (2) being overly condescending and indicating bias within the body of their initial, official report, (3) intentional coaching of key witnesses interviewed by Air Force personnel, and (4) the obvious disregard of interviews with key personnel involved or witnesses to portions of the event—all of whom are now deceased.

Since the very moment Marcel returned to the RAAF in 1947, this investigation has been fueled by facts and falsehoods, by sworn testimony and perjury, with hoaxes and lies. It began with the announcement of divulged operational intelligence in the form of a press release created by none other than Roswell Army Airfield counterintelligence officials with the intent to dilute, distract, and diffuse the facts of the events. Intentionally, they created what we would now call "fake news" in order to confuse any additional inquiries into the actual happenings at the Foster Ranch and possibly other locations in the area where wreckage, debris, or a flying disk was recovered.

Was it the crash of a "flying disk"? Was it the crash of a "flying saucer"? An extraterrestrial vehicle manned with aliens?

Was there a midair collision that brought the material down? Was the Foster Ranch site evidence of a mere initial impact and the vehicle actually came to rest at a different location? Was it the effects of a lightning storm that caused an aerial explosion? Was it a midair collision? Was it a top-secret US military experiment? An experimental aircraft crash? A nuclear incident? A Manhattan-like project testing time travel or invisibility technologies? Could it have been an experiment that was conducted even above the airfield generals' heads, like an aerial vehicle created by former German engineers and scientists at Alamogordo or somewhere else? These and many other theories continue to be explored and all for exceptionally good reasons.

Brigadier General Thomas DuBose admitted as much and was quoted in *UFO Crash at Roswell* by Kevin Randle and Don Schmitt. DuBose's interview can be viewed on YouTube.

General McMullen

"It was a cover story—the balloon part of it... It's the story to be given to the press and that is it and anything else, forget it. And McMullen if you ever knew him you told him—if he wanted to run something, he Goddamn sure ran it. He knew every facet of the operation—he was a busybody. He wanted to know what the hell was going on, who was pissing on the sidewalk and all that sort of thing.

"McMullen told me, 'You are not to discuss this and this is a point in which—this is more than top secret. It's beyond that. It's within my priority as deputy to George Kenny, and he in turn responsible to the President—this is the highest priority you could exhibit and you will say nothing,' and that was the end of it."

Brigadier General Thomas DuBose (Ret.)

General DuBose was the highest-ranking officer involved in the Roswell Incident who ever agreed to go on record about the story.

In 1947, DuBose was the chief of staff for General Roger Ramey, the commanding officer of the 8th Air Force at Fort Worth Army Airfield (FWAA) later renamed Carswell Air Force Base. DuBose was an integral part of arranging for the recovered Roswell debris to be flown to FWAA along with arranging the meeting with Maj. Jesse Marcel and the subsequent famous photos for the *Fort Worth Star-Telegram.*

DuBose was a man deeply involved in managing the incident, which begs the question, why did the 1995 United States Air Force report not seriously consider DuBose's testimony? Why would they completely downplay this key figure in the Roswell puzzle? Why would they continue to dilute, distract, and diffuse the information gathered by scores of individual investigators?

The 1994/95 official account titled *The Roswell Report – Fact versus Fiction in the New Mexico Desert*, compiled by the headquarters of the US Air Force, was an example of yet another attempt by the Air Force, or possibly other government officials, to hide sensitive intelligence information or maybe to hide something else. The question is what? What could be so top secret that the Air Force would continue its deception five decades later? After all, this report came out forty-eight years after the incident occurred, and four years after the complete dissolution of the Soviet Union. What would be the point of continuing to deny a spy program conducted by NYC college kids out of Alamogordo? What would be the reason the Air Force would want to continue to distract from the overall investigation by later adding aerial parachute test dummies as an explanation for accounts of extraterrestrial bodies? Using an Air Force pilot with a head injury as an explanation of aliens described with unusually large heads?

To put the case material into perspective, you must consider the United States declassification process, the method in which government entities either withhold or disseminate categories of information. Declassification is when government entities cease the restriction of information, at which time it can be accessed by the public through the Freedom of Information Act (FOIA). Sensitive information is subject to mandatory declassification review and by default will be declassified after ten years. Declassification is automatic after twenty-five years with nine exceptions that allow the restriction to the material to continue. Beyond fifty years, there are only two allowances. Anything more takes special permission. At this point, what are they concealing that would warrant granting this? What could be so important that special permission has been given to continue to withhold this information? It's not a weather balloon, and it makes no sense the government would continue hiding anything related to the MOGUL balloon experiments.

At what point does an investigator decide that the provider of the information has been so deceptive, condescending, and disingenuous that no matter what they say in future interviews or written disseminations, they must be considered an untruthful entity? What acts would they have committed to deem secrecy for such an extended period of time?

In most criminal cases there are two reasons why a person commits the offense. One is considered a general motive, and the other is a specialized motive. A generalized motive occurs when someone commits an offense such as theft, burglary, and robbery. Their motive is to obtain someone else's property for their own gain. Specialized motive is committed for specific personal reasons such as hatred for the victim, retribution, or to cast blame—an individually specialized intent. It would seem in the Roswell Incident we have multiple motives for the cover-up of whatever occurred and for the continued smokescreen presented by the Air Force to confuse current and future investigators.

When examining the Roswell Incident, researchers must take into consideration the political environment in 1947 Eastern Europe. At the conclusion of World War II and with the redrawing of countries' borders, the newly empowered political classes begin essentially playing political chess. The Soviet Union slowly began to claim other nations along its border in this new postwar world. America was genuinely concerned about this. They were so concerned that they started radio broadcasts that would reach into the Eastern Bloc, trying to sell American democratic beliefs and values. Due to the aggression of the Soviet Union and their posturing, the United States began working on what would be later called the Marshall Plan enacted in 1948. It was during 1947 that the United States began serious considerations for attempting to stop the spread of communism. The idea behind the Marshall Plan was to infuse western European countries with funding, bring down trade barriers, and provide for rapid economic recovery after the war. This would ally these countries with the United States and limit Soviet expansion.

In the case of national security, it is completely understandable that a government, in order to protect their population to various degrees, would want to conceal information of a sensitive nature. They would want to eliminate possible exposure that could harm their cause. I understand if a secret project called MOGUL intended to listen for Soviet bomb test detonations, conducted by personnel of New York College operating out of Alamogordo, it would need to be guarded. But after confirmation that the Soviets had the capabilities to create a nuclear weapon, what would be the point of secrecy—the Soviets knew we were watching and listening, they were watching and listening as well.

Why continue the deception?

In the case of Roswell, General DuBose is a perfect example of the government's continued efforts and dishonesty. DuBose was not a detached witness. He was an eyewitness to the organization of the cover-up, an eyewitness to the dissemination of a false narrative, an eyewitness to the transport of the suspected material, and an eyewitness to a staged photo operation intended to be released to the *Fort Worth Star-Telegram* and AP services.

Of all of the witnesses interviewed by Kevin Randal, Don Schmitt, Tom Carey, and many other investigators, it is my opinion that the most important testimony to the Air Force's deception came from General DuBose. The problem is that he remained obscure in his suggestions and refused to define in any detailed specifics of what the cover story was protecting.

Can you imagine keeping a secret of such magnitude all these years? What could be, in General DuBose own words: "... *more than top secret. It's beyond that.*"?

What is more than top secret?

Throughout this book, I will refer to sections of witness affidavits, and we will examine their importance and meaning. The real problem with transcribing an affidavit is it truly is not in and affiant's (the witness's) own words. Typically, if the investigator has little experience and is using only a standardized template they read about in a book or learned in a basic police or military interview course they completed, they are excluding subtle, latent, and unintentional information that may lead the investigator down a more productive trail or may indicate signs of deception.

Statement analysis, as portrayed and criticized on the internet, does not prove guilt or innocence—it is merely an additional evaluation tool to be used in conjunction with the techniques of interviewing, passive cross-examining, and if required, interrogation. Coupled with understanding these skills, a comprehensive investigator should incorporate the cognitive interview and, if trained, a regressive interview.

But I understand the purpose of a sanitized and concise sworn statement—it is just for the facts, ma'am. In the DuBose affidavit (Randle) you can review online, the investigators established the following details and had the general swear an oath that the statement was true and correct to the best of his knowledge:

1. Established his legal name.
2. Established his current address.
3. Established his overall career history.
4. Established he was an Air Force colonel assigned to the Fort Worth Army Airfield (FWAA) at the time of the incident.
5. Established by order of General McMullen, DuBose phoned Colonel Blanchard and ordered the recovered material to be sent to him in Fort Worth.
6. Established that DuBose had FWAA commander

Colonel Clark fly the material to General McMullen, who in turn said he would send it to General Benjamin Chidlaw at Wright Field.

7. Established the photographed material was from a weather balloon.
8. Established DuBose did not receive material gain for his statement.

But even in a sanitized statement such as the DuBose affidavit, there are still things that can be discovered or theorized about the circumstances surrounding the cover-up. The following are several additional facts that we can identify from this transcribed statement:

1. General McMullen was the highest-ranking officer involved, therefore was managing the conspiracy or at least approved the diversion of facts and official actions.
2. As late as 1991, DuBose still believed the material was sent to McMullen and later on to Wright Patterson. This contradicts Ramey's statement from other witnesses of cancelling the flights forwarding the material.
3. The material in the photos taken by J. Bond Johnson of the *Fort Worth Star-Telegram* was not the material brought to Fort Worth by Marcel.

Reviewing actions and statements after planned operations is an integral part of the overall effectiveness of the mission—this technique provides a list of lessons learned. Also, it's as important at the end of your day, if you cannot identify at least three mistakes you made during your past waking hours, you are probably untrainable. Unfortunately, mistakes are our best teachers—you learn little and are impressed upon less impactfully when you are simply correct in actions and assumptions and move on. Spending the time on cool reflection in reference to your mistake and determining a better course of action to be used the next time you are faced with a similar challenge is the entire goal of debriefing and after-action reviews.

I realize by revisiting some of these interviews and portions of the Roswell investigation there will be those who will attack me on what they perceived to be my lack of knowledge of the subject. My inability to follow every clue perfectly to see what they deem to be the big picture. I realize there are those who irrationally see conspiracy in everything involving the government. I accept the fact that there will be those who do not understand what a debriefing is for. What an after-action report intends to address. How boiling down an incomprehensibly complex set of events and analyzing the bare bones for lessons learned is a worthy endeavor. Because, bottom line, the most important facet of this book is to not repeat our same mistakes again and again. Yes, our mistakes—the Roswell investigators as a whole, including the government. If we don't critically examine our mistakes, identify the distractions that lead us down the wrong trails, we will never get to the truth.

There are so many things to consider when reviewing the Roswell Incident. Persons implicated, testimony given, circumstances concerned, locations involved, and all of the intentional false testimony. The false assumption that many inexperienced researchers of the Roswell Incident make: if someone lies to you once, their entire testimony is discredited. This cannot be further from the truth. Many criminal cases that I have investigated involved persons of questionable character. During official interviews with numerous suspects, I observed dozens of cues of deception. However, throughout the investigation I later discovered these cues were not related to the actual crime at all; however, the person I was interviewing was simply trying to hide other criminal offenses they took part in or were aware of.

Standard deceptive speech patterns and body language alone does not prove anything; they must be identified as related to the circumstances.

It appears that to the day he died, Gen. DuBose believed the material brought from the Foster Ranch to Fort Worth was later transported to other military facilities for identification and further analysis. In support of this, Sappho Henderson, wife of pilot Oliver "Pappy" Henderson, relayed that he had told her he was the one who flew the material to Wright Field. Several other former pilots who served with Henderson reported him speaking about possibly taking the material to Wright Field.

I believe Brigadier General Thomas DuBose to be a good and honest man, a war hero, and a patriot. I believe the decisions he made while in uniform were based on his understanding of what is best for the country and in line with the orders of his superior officers. Did he deceive the citizens of the United States? Yes. Did he conspire to divert attention away from the facts of the Roswell Incident? Yes. Was there malicious intent in the action he took? I say no.

At the end of his life, General DuBose came forward and admitted to the people of the United State the nature of his deception and the involvement of his dishonesty. However, there is one thing that he maintained—the true secret of what he was actually concealing.

2

THE STRUGGLE OF MAJOR JESSE MARCEL

FORMER INTELLIGENCE OFFICER 509TH BOMB GROUP ROSWELL ARMY AIRFIELD

Major Jesse Marcel

EVERY GOOD CONSPIRACY NEEDS A COVER-UP, AND EVERY good cover-up needs a fall man. Intelligence Officer Major Jesse Marcel was the perfect target for both. Just based on his facial expressions during the famous photo session in Fort Worth, you can imagine as he stood in the office of General George Ramey, commanding officer for the Eighth Air Force at Fort Worth Army Airfield, he began to realize what was happening.

Marcel had reported recovering material from a "flying disk" in the high desert of New Mexico to his base commander Col. Blanchard. He identified the fragments as quote: "... not being from this Earth..." He had secretly shown the material to his eleven-year-old son, Jessie Marcel, Jr., and his wife before bringing the debris to the RAAF for official inspection. He had briefed his chain of command and the public information officer (PIO) Lieutenant Walter Haut of his findings and his determination. He had read the original press briefing in the *Roswell Daily Record* with no dispute. And then he personally escorted the strange material to the Fort Worth Army Airfield at Ramey's instruction.

It was then everything changed.

After joining Ramey in his office and showing the material to the general, according to Marcel, Ramey asked him to go with him to a map room and show him exactly where the wreckage was found. Marcel did so, and when he and Ramey returned to the general's office, the original material Marcel had brought had been replaced with material from a standard weather balloon.

Shortly after, General Ramey, Colonel Thomas DuBose, Warrant Officer Irving Newton, *Fort Worth Star-Telegram* photographer James Bond Johnson, and Marcel posed for pictures in Ramey's office. Marcel later stated he realized the wreckage had been replaced but at the time remained a good soldier and followed his superior's instructions. He was given his orders by Ramey to take part in the photo session and to say nothing that the material used in the photos was not what he had originally found or brought to him.

Today, many citizens of the United States, if they were put in this position and believed the material they found was extraterrestrial, would immediately leak the information and/or become a whistleblower. In 1947, two years after WWII and in the beginning of the Cold War with the Soviets, the punishment for such actions could be the death penalty. Although rarely used today, federal capital punishment can be imposed for many things along with espionage and treason. This would have been the case had Major Marcel released the truth to the public. The last espionage execution in the United States occurred on June 19, 1953, about seven years after the Roswell Incident. Husband and wife Julius and Ethel Rosenberg were executed by electric chair for being convicted of passing atomic secrets to the Soviet Union. The situation Marcel faced was not to be taken lightly—he could lose his life.

Afterwards, Marcel stood watching as military personnel gathered up the material Ramey had staged—the materials of a common weather balloon. Within moments, all the material was gone, and Marcel's head was spinning. He had not quite processed what he had just been a member of—or an accomplice in. Later he would clearly understand that he, Jesse Marcel, was the key focus in what would become the most famous UFO conspiracy in the United States, possibly the world.

Once briefed by Ramey to remain silent on the matter, he was dismissed. He walked across and out of the office. You can imagine how the world around him quieted as his brain went into overdrive processing the whole spectacle. This confusion and his subsequent battle of knowing the truth but not being able to speak it disturbed him for years. The shiny foil of the radar reflectors, the thin wood sticks use for their framing, and the rubber material of the weather balloon. All, according to Marcel, substituted for the real debris—the actual items recovered from the site.

Marcel was the intelligence officer for the 509th Bomb Wing at RAAF. He was in charge of a department of approximately five officers, both intelligence and counterintelligence, and around twenty enlisted personnel. While his main job at the 509th was clearing assigned personnel through the Atomic Energy Commission, he was also a man who knew how to get secrets, how to keep secrets, and how to cover up secrets. He realized this was the common link of the entire operation—their entire plan. He felt flush, his stomach heavy; this culpability seemed to press down on him for decades to come.

The official stories printed in the *Roswell Daily Record* for July 8 and July 9, 1947, would stand as the explanation of the incident for the next thirty-one years. While there were additional stories written in other papers, the basic information shared and accuracy of the Roswell events did not improve; therefore there is no reason to address subsequent AP articles listed in so many other books and online. It's like playing the story carousel game—each time the story is retold, it changes slightly and usually gets further from the truth.

The initial newspaper's accounts were simply that a lowly sheep rancher named W. W. "Mac" (Mack) Brazel notified Chaves County Sheriff George Wilcox that he had found some strange debris on the Foster Ranch northwest of Roswell. He thought it might be material from some of the reported mysterious "flying disks" reported seen throughout the country and there may be a reward. Because of the military activity in the area, the sheriff had notified the Roswell Army Airfield (RAAF) and the 509th Bomb Wing intelligence officer Major Jesse Marcel. Major Marcel had accompanied Brazel out to the ranch, where debris was collected, and determined it to part from a reported "flying disk." The following day, Marcel accompanied the material to the Fort Worth Army Airfield, where he met with General George Ramey and conducted a press conference of sorts. Photos were taken of Major Marcel, Colonel DuBose, and General Ramey posing with the material, now reidentified per Ramey's orders as common weather balloon fragments.

Case closed...

Later, Major Marcel made his way back to the flight line and boarded his plane for the flight back to Roswell. You can imagine as the plane took off, he tried to settle in and get some sleep on the way back, but his mind was on overload. What did it all mean? How would he ever get past being the intelligence officer who misidentified a spacecraft from another planet as a common weather balloon?

Later in life he would discover that the answer to that question was: Never.

It is truly unfortunate that the fate of Jesse Marcel was sealed with this incident—at least in his own mind. He intended to complete a full career with the US Army Air Forces; however within a short time after the incident, he separated from the military. Many Roswell investigators and theorist have suggested that the incident somehow marred his career, and he left disgruntled, the fall guy of a ridiculous tale of spaceships and weather balloons. However, with well-done research, this does not appear to be the case—family obligations seem to be the real purpose for his departure from the military. His service to the United States Army Air Forces and assignment to the 509th Bomb Wing was a true source of pride for him, and that would never change—neither would his original story. He maintained for the rest of his life and in the 1980, season 5, episode 1 of the TV show *In Search Of* that the material found on the Foster Ranch was "*not anything from this Earth.*"

Years later, the deception portrayed in the photos taken at Fort Worth weighed on his conscience. It weighed on him so much to the point of violating his oath of secrecy to the US Army Air Forces, and he went against the direct orders he'd received from General Ramey that day in July 1947.

Knowing that he was still judged by some service personnel as the US Army Air Forces intelligence officer who could not tell the difference between an extraterrestrial spacecraft and a common weather balloon, Marcel became entrenched in the efforts of clearing his name and bringing truth to the event. But, not only clearing the stigma placed on his name by General Ramey and their entire upper chain of command—he wanted to tell the world that we are not alone.

While he was not necessarily completely consumed by this idea, he refused to take family and friend's advice to just let it go. He felt it important enough and worthy enough for the truth to be told. He knew in his heart, the items he'd found on the Foster Ranch were significant enough to possibly change the human perception of the world.

By 1978, former Army Air Forces Major Jesse Marcel could hold this deception in no longer. He began speaking in public about the events that took place on the Foster Ranch and his involvement in collecting the crashed materials there—approximately seventy-five miles northwest of Roswell.

Marcel repeated much of the Roswell Incident story that was already spoken of on the local radio stations and printed in the local papers in 1947. However, there were several facts of the event that were either excluded or changed to fit the security requirements and narrative of the US government.

Marcel confirmed that later in the afternoon of Sunday, July 6, 1947, he and RAAF counterintelligence officer Captain Sheridan Cavitt followed Mack Brazel out to the Foster Ranch, approximately thirty miles southeast of Corona. They arrived late and slept overnight in the Hines House, a small cabin Brazel used while he was staying overnight on the property. This is something Cavitt would later publicly dispute. However, Marcel said the next morning the three men went to the location of the debris field and started collecting the materials from what appeared to be a crash site.

Today, in the case of an aerial vehicle crash, the Air Force Safety and Accident Board investigative standards would at minimum require proper visual documentation and photos, impact and structural measurements, technical inspections, and a survey of the area to be completed before any wreckage is moved or recovered.

In 1947, things were different.

To understand, we need to take a look at 1941, the year the United States Army Air Corps became the United States Army Air Forces (Army Air Forces). By 1942 they had created the Office of Flying Safety to deal with the substantial increase of aircraft accidents. In the previous year, the Army Air Corps had evolved into accepting what some critics would call "leisurely practices." But in the beginning of America's involvement in WWII, thousands of planes were being constructed; therefore thousands of men had to crew them. This put extreme pressure on personnel selection and pilot training (Pierce XV).

In the following years after assimilating these new pilots, there was a huge increase of accidents and fatalities. In 1939, the Army Air Corps had pinned flying wings on just 1,000 pilots—by 1943, they had pinned flying wings on 165,000 pilots, and the statistics of this incredible increase are disturbing. During WWII, the US suffered over 52,000 aircrew combat deaths and lost over 22,000 aircraft. The shocking fact is that over 21,000 aircraft were lost due to noncombat accidents within the borders of the United States and over 20,000 in accidents overseas (Pierce). The accidents within the US borders alone equated to over 15,000 fatalities (Blanchard). These enormous losses fueled a change within the US Army Air Forces and later brought about a new organizational philosophy of professionalism and safety.

Today, the citizens of the United States cannot even imagine accepting these staggering losses of service personnel in war, not to mention in training. However, between 1941 and 1945, the war took precedence over the safety of airmen's lives. It is crazy to think this was accepted, but it was truly a different time, and American citizens understood to defeat the military aggression of the countries of Germany and Japan, sacrifices would have to be made. And the Army Air Corps paid the price of over 88,000 airmen killed (Amer. Leg.).

During this period, commanders in charge of operational airfields referred to "Army Air Forces Regulation 62-14, Reporting and Investigation of Aircraft Accidents." This guide set forth the policies to be followed in the event of an accident involving any aircraft. Additionally, most airfields had what would be considered outlined standard operating procedures (SOP), or sometimes referred to as local flying regulations, a smaller set of guidelines explaining how the assigned personnel are to conduct their responsibilities within the Army Air Forces' regulations.

Regulation 62-14 for investigations had several mandates; however, I will only address those that would relate to the Roswell Incident. Along with many other conditions, 62-14 required each airfield to (1) establish an Aircraft Accident Committee, (2) conclude that the deputy for Maintenance and Supply will be responsible for the disposition of the wreckage, (3) that a technical inspector would complete the 62-14 checklist in section II prior to moving the wreckage, and (4) the chain of command is to be immediately notified.

It appears, based on historical documents and eyewitness testimony, the only requirement of 62-14 completed by Colonel Blanchard was notifying his immediate chain of command. Subsequently, he ordered his intelligence officer and a counterintelligence officer to respond to the Foster Ranch and clean up the debris field. Based on the amount of aircraft accidents experienced by the Army Air Forces during Blanchard's service, and the fact that he was the airfield's commanding officer, it can be deduced that he was well versed in aircraft accident procedures, specifically regulation 62-14, and did not believe the debris field located on the Foster Ranch was related to any kind of aircraft accident, friendly or otherwise. At this point, most people with interest in the Roswell Incident have conceded that the debris on the Foster Ranch was not that of a US aircraft, missile, or any other apparatus of that type. If Blanchard had initially thought it could be a US flying machine of some sort, he would have informed and mobilized the required assets according to the 62-14 regulation.

He did not do this.

He sent his intelligence and counterintelligence officers out. Men with the training and knowledge to identify craft and materials that were friend or foe, and with the training and knowledge to conceal and/or confuse any additional parties who were to inquire deeper into what these military men recovered out there in the desert.

Most of what is described in the PIO's press release, even the account that was translated and published by the *Roswell Daily Record*, seems a reasonable response for the RAAF. The real question I have is what Major Marcel did on his way back to the RAAF. Using the argument that the men of the 509th were hand selected, and Jesse Marcel was such a trusted officer with a high-level security clearance, why would he take unknown material, perhaps classified material, possibly contaminated material, into his home and allow his wife and eleven-year-old son to handle it?

Things that make you go hmmm…

3

KENNETH ARNOLD AND THE MISSING C-46

UFO WITNESS AND PRIVATE PILOT FROM BOISE, IDAHO

Kenneth Arnold

IT IS DIFFICULT, IF NOT IMPOSSIBLE FOR PEOPLE OF THE twenty-first century to imagine or understand what it was like living day to day in the 1940s. While you can read books and watch movies, one still cannot master the emotions of the times, the perception of the world as American citizens accepted it, and the cultural coping mechanisms regular people relied on, such as US citizens' majority belief in God, trust in government affairs, and strong personal bonds with family, friends, and community. All of which in the twenty-first century are fractured.

At the time of the 1947 Roswell Incident, the United States was still healing wounds inflicted from four years of war with Germany and Japan. By the end of World War II on September 2, 1945, there were estimated nearly eighty-five million people worldwide who perished as a result of the fighting (World Pop.). These estimates vary by about twenty million depending on the source. But one thing is constant, civilian deaths double the military deaths and more, in every source estimate. The United States alone lost over four hundred thousand service personnel, which didn't even compare to the Soviets' losses of between eight and eleven million. Most of these humans were buried in mass graves, cremated, or buried randomly in unmarked graves.

Erased from the memory of the world.

As nations were preoccupied with healing and rebuilding, the machines of war and justice remained active. Militaries globally were rebuilding, reorganizing, and realigning with their new allies and redefining their military branches' various missions. The Nuremberg Trials were underway in Germany in an attempt to bring Nazi war criminals to justice (Nur. Trial). Of those charged, eleven officers and Nazi political officials and supporters were put to death by hanging. In conjunction, General Douglas MacArthur established the International Military Tribunal for the Far East, also referred to as the Tokyo War Crime Tribunal. Twenty-eight Japanese leaders and military personnel were prosecuted by the United States. The US prosecutor oversaw the convictions, executing seven military officials and civilian leaders of the Empire of Japan. However, there were many other minor tribunals overseen by various interested parties that resulted in over one thousand executions for alleged war crimes (Intl. Mil. Tri. Far East).

During this time, the Soviet Union was becoming increasingly paranoid about Western interference with their communist doctrine and made drastic efforts in hardening their borders. Knowing this, the allied countries expedited many of the judicial resolutions along with border disputes in a further attempt to isolate the Soviets and provide stability in Europe and the Far East.

While the United States had suffered greatly during the war, it was nothing compared to the murder and devastation suffered in Europe. Back in America, veterans were returning to civilian life, the economy was strengthening, and the remaining military service personnel were having to adjust to the massive personnel downsizing. Deactivation of entire military units and support structures, and the reallocation of unit designations the government intended to leave in place was the order of the day.

It was during this transitional time that the United States Army Air Forces was given the mandate for re-designation as the United States Air Force, effective September 18, 1947. The year leading up to the split was a year of flux from new policies, new equipment, new procedures, and a complete reorganization of personnel. Roswell Army Airfield was no different. During the summer of 1946, the RAAF was re-designated from the 509th Composite Group (the airwing that delivered the nuclear bombs to Hiroshima and Nagasaki) to the 509th Bombardment Group, Very Heavy—now commonly known as the 509th Bomb Wing. At that time, it was the only nuclear-capable military organization in the world. The Soviets knew this, and through their paranoia, the arms race was on.

At this point the Soviets as well as the rest of the world knew that the United States had nuclear weapons, and furthermore they knew the United States would use them if forced to. The experiences with recent modern warfare had catapulted the world into a newer and deadlier arena of war machine design and tactics evolution. This entire environment, along with the United States' controversial program Operation Paperclip, deluged an already tense situation with additional reasons of mistrust and suspicion.

Operation Paperclip was carried out by US Army Counterintelligence Corps special agents, in which over 1,600 German scientific and technology professionals were brought to the United States and employed by the US government for special and classified projects—mainly creating machines of war (Lewis). The program brought to America men such as former SS Nazi and V-2 Rocket scientist Kurt Debus, who later became the first director of NASA's Launch Operations Center along with V-2 Rocket developer Wernher von Braun (Biography), who became the chief architect of the NASA Apollo Saturn V rocket program ("Launching a Vision"). Debus, von Braun, and hundreds of others were assigned and distributed throughout the United States to work in labs and on test projects for the US government. These former Nazi scientists and engineers were embedded into the workings of the government and transplanted into US society.

Many such scientists and engineers were sent to places like Alamogordo and White Sands, New Mexico, and later to the famous Area 51 to develop and test aircraft, weaponry, and classified surveillance equipment. New Mexico and Nevada were the perfect places for such development to be pursued. They are very remote, sparsely populated and easy to control. These areas would limit citizens' exposure to experimental activities along with minimizing potential collateral damages that may come out of weaponry and aerial tests and/or malfunctions of the same.

Government programs like Operation Paperclip and the tales of WWII aerial phenomena such as Foo Fighters, glowing orbs that would follow flying military aircraft witnessed over

Germany, and stories told in mass-marketed pulp magazines led to America's paranoia about the Soviet Union and increased the average citizen's tendency to watch the sky more closely (Krazney). Only a few years after the war, citizens of Europe were also reporting "Ghost Airplanes" and "Ghost Rockets" in the northern reaches of Norway and Denmark (Liljegren).

And when Americans looked, they saw.

During 1947, there were hundreds of UFO reports throughout the United States. One of the most notable reported UFO sightings would come from Kenneth Arnold of Boise, Idaho. On June 24, 1947, days before the Roswell Incident was reported, Kenneth was flying himself on a business trip at approximately 9,200 feet from Chehalis, Washington, to Yakima, Washington. His route would lead him by Mount Rainier, where on December 10, 1946, a Marine Corps C-46 Curtis Commando transport plane had gone down with thirty-two Marines on board and had yet to be located. Because of a $5,000 reward for the plane, he decided to make a brief detour and make an attempt to locate the downed aircraft. Somewhere near Mineral, Washington, Arnold changed course back to his original destination of Yakima. Within a few minutes Arnold noticed bright silver flashes of light off to his left, back near Mount Rainier. Initially he believed these flashes to be reflections or some sort of optical illusion off of his eyeglasses or aircraft windows. He removed his glasses and rolled down the window, confirming that these lights were no reflections. He described them as moving incredibly fast. He later reported to airport officials in Yakima, at approximately 3:00 p.m. he sighted up to nine shiny UFOs. They were bright silver and shaped like a modified batwing. This was the first official UFO sighting in the United States since after World War II. Using the training he received as a pilot, he watched the objects travel between Mount Rainier and Mount Adams, then determined their speed to be up to an astonishing 1,700 mph. Later,

Kenneth continued his flight to Pendleton, Oregon, where he attended an air show.

The next day, on June 25, Kenneth was interviewed by reporter from the *East Oregonian* newspaper in Pendleton. It was there he described the craft that he saw was rounded in the front and chopped in the back, coming to a point, similar to a bat wing. It was during this interview that the information got a little modified by the reporter. According to Arnold, the UFOs were not a perfect saucer or disk shape. In later years he was insistent that he described them as like a crescent moon and that they moved like saucers skipping on water. Whatever the actual description was, the newspapers of the day began describing these aerial objects as "flying saucers" or "flying disks."

Thus, the flying saucer phenomenon was born.

Over the next several months, his story in the media had small changes, and ultimately, he had to clarify the shape of the objects that he saw. He went on record describing the craft as crescent shaped and not as discs, contrary to what many media outlets were suggesting. And apparently the media stuck with saucers...

In the 1950s and 1960s, there were hundreds of reports by citizens and investigations conducted by government and Air Force personnel. These were the occurrences that brought the world into the age of the flying saucer and pitting investigators against one another. The decades after the Roswell Incident bore multiple factions and many differing schools of thought. Many of the extraterrestrial skeptics passionately believed any UFO reported phenomena could be easily explained as manmade aircraft or natural phenomenon—they completely dismissed any other possibilities to the point of condemnation of those who disagreed. Because of the lack of evidence put forward from the burgeoning ufology community, the skeptics seemed to win the day, explaining that many of the sightings were attributed to meteors, the planet Venus, far-off manmade aircraft, optical illusions, and in the case of my UFO sighting when I was five years old, a high-altitude weather balloon.

Oddly enough, while these debates raged, the United States Air Force was under a mandate to investigate these reports. The Roswell Incident had been so well camouflaged, it was never included in the review.

It was never even considered...

In 1948 Project Sign was implemented by Air Force General Nathan Twining of the Air Technical Service Command. Initially called Project Saucer, the program was tasked with evaluating UFO reports to determine if they were a threat to national security. Oddly enough, when the Air Force investigators of Project Sign concluded that the UFO phenomenon was attributed to extraterrestrials, the powers that be closed down the program, replacing it with Project Grudge. Project Grudge resulted in a poorly funded and mismanaged endeavor that was noticeably short lived and therefore resulted in the creation of Project Bluebook.

Project Bluebook's original director, Captain Edward Ruppelt, initially started the program, and it operated for the next eighteen years. J. Allen Hynek, also with Sign and Grudge, remained as a scientific consultant under the program and investigated hundreds of UFO reports. The conclusion was (1) they could neither prove nor disprove the extraterrestrial hypothesis, (2) the findings did not lead to any observed craft performance indications above that regular manned flight could accomplish, and (3) the events investigated did not appear to be any threat to national security.

Bluebook was completely shut down by 1970.

Probably...

And like Project Bluebook, the Roswell Army Airfield had its beginning, a middle, and an end. You see, the airfield was originally opened on September 20, 1941, as the Roswell Army Air Corps flying school. Desolate, flat, and known for its good weather, it was a perfect place for new pilots to earn their wings. Its name soon changed to the Roswell Army Airfield, and then in late 1947 to the Roswell Air Force Base. It wasn't until 1948 that it received its proper name, Walker Air Force Base, named after New Mexico native and Congressional Medal of Honor recipient General Kenneth Walker. Unfortunately, the Air Force Base was closed in 1967, just shy of twenty years old.

Now, absorbed by the City of Roswell, just remnants of the military presence remain. A couple of hangars, a small control tower, a few scatter buildings and the runways are all that lingers of the original airfield. Currently known as the Roswell International Air Center, the tarmac and runways are lined with over two hundred huge, decommissioned commercial passenger jets from a variety of airlines, just waiting to be scrapped or cannibalized for replacement parts. A sad legacy for such a once prestigious facility.

Seeing the dilapidated and dusty complex as it is today, it's hard to imagine at one time the complex had armed guards at the gates, housed thousands of military and civilian workers, hundreds of vehicles and aircraft, barracks buildings, maintenance facilities, administrative offices, a hospital, and supported a military organization that for a time possessed the most powerful weapons in the world.

The 509th Bomb Wing.

4

THE ELUSIVE COLONEL WILLIAM "BUTCH" BLANCHARD

FORMER COMMANDING OFFICER 509TH BOMB GROUP
ROSWELL ARMY AIRFIELD

Colonel William "Butch" Blanchard

IF YOU EVER WANTED TO USE A PERSON AS A SPECIFIC example of what a military officer should be, you can look to none other than General William Blanchard. He was a true hero. During World War II, Blanchard was the deputy commander of the 58th Bomb Wing. The 58th was the unit that was first assigned to fly B-29 Superfortresses into China, providing bombing and air support against Imperial Japan.

35

These aircraft were the most advanced in the US military's arsenal, and the men who flew them were highly professional and the most qualified. By the end of World War II, Blanchard's decorations included the Distinguished Service Medal, the Silver Star, multiple Bronze Stars, and the Air Medal to name a few. He was the epitome of a true patriot, dedicated officer, and servant of the United States. And it's because of these reasons I find it so hard to stand and point my finger and accuse this man of lying to his country. But like many other people who understand conflict, who are educated in warfare, and who are experienced in the matters of military operational secrecy, I understand why he did what he did—it is the reasons that surround his deception that become obscure.

Blanchard had a distinguished military career. He graduated the United States Military Academy at West Point in 1938. Serving in the United States Army Air Corps, he conducted his flight training at Randolph and Kelly fields in Texas. He later held positions as a flight instructor and the chief of advanced pilot training. After the war, Blanchard was later assigned to the 509th Bomb Wing at Roswell. During the transition time from 1946 to about 1948, he participated in nuclear bomb testing in Operation Crossroads on the Bikini Atoll and was also assigned as the commander of the Roswell Army Airfield. This was a huge responsibility, since the 509th Bomb Wing was the only nuclear-capable bomb wing in the world at the time. The responsibility of such an assignment is unfathomable.

With that amount of personnel, equipment, and strategic responsibility, disaster could strike at any time and from any direction. That is why I find it incredibly interesting how little a role Colonel Blanchard played in the Roswell Incident. There is extraordinarily little documentation that would determine where Blanchard was and what he was engaging with in the early days of July 1947. Oftentimes in a criminal investigation, it is what is missing that is the biggest clue. And in the case of Roswell, that would be the lack of records and documentation during this time.

When investigating modern major crimes such as homicides, home invasions, and sex crimes, investigators rely heavily on technology. Prior to cell phones and the internet, there was a huge emphasis on learning interview and interrogation techniques. Today's investigators rely more on technology such as computer searches, database mining, and cell phone records—none of which were available at the time of the Roswell Incident.

To clarify, in 1947 the first transistor was invented, which later gave way to advances in computing. However, in 1947, the primary mode of official military communications was via radio, teletype, and voice landline telephone. It appears just based on the general information provided by witnesses and other involved persons, most of the Roswell Incident communication was conducted either face-to-face or by telephone. Neither of which generates any records.

In today's cases, a suspect's whereabouts are often determined based on their cell phone data, GPS information, and the cell towers that were activated during the use of the suspect's cell phone, or just the cell phone's proximity to the tower. In the case of Colonel Blanchard around the week of July 4, it was reported that he was conveniently off base by July 9. It was reported that by July 8, the staff of the 509th Bomb Wing informed anyone inquiring about Colonel Blanchard's whereabouts that he was on leave. Given the suspected nature of the events that were transpiring in the Roswell region at that time (a downed UFO), it is highly suspect that Colonel Blanchard would actually go on leave.

While there are many Roswell investigators who have their hypothesis of what the colonel was doing, I can say given the documents and facts as they have been presented in history and throughout the works of many investigators, we actually do not know exactly where he was or what he was doing. Blanchard could have been on leave, he could have documented that he was on leave and actually been supervising additional recovery efforts related to the material found on the Foster Ranch, or he could have been doing any number of other things.

For Colonel Blanchard to simply release information on recovering a controversial flying disc, and then leave the area borderlines on the ridiculous—but if Blanchard really didn't feel this event (reported by some investigators as the most important event in human history) was important enough to stick around, then he certainly had the authority to take leave. And this would seem to be the case. Based on the RAAF daily morning reports Colonel Blanchard's leave was documented as July 9 through July 26. That's as accurate as we can get based on official written documentation.

Colonel Blanchard's second in command, Colonel Payne Jennings, was more than capable of handling the situation and could easily have been available for questions from the media. Colonel Jennings has been implicated by Roswell investigators in the Roswell Incident cover-up; however, there is little documentation to support it. Yet, like Blanchard, Ramey and other command staff officers, Colonel Jennings was never interviewed. Within four years of the Roswell Incident, on March 29, 1951, the B-29 Superfortress Jennings was flying in had a catastrophic malfunction that ultimately resulted in the premature detonation of the 12,000-pound Tarzon bomb they were carrying—the aircraft, material, and all crew were lost in the East China Sea, northwest of Okinawa while en route to a target, Sinuiju, Korea (AMS-A-1).

They were never recovered—their remains never located.

The second thing I find extremely interesting about Colonel William Blanchard is his rocketing success even after the Roswell flying saucer fiasco. Whenever I'm engaged in a presentation or just a conversation with someone about the Roswell Incident, I always fall back on this simple line of logic. If you were the boss and one of your employees did a press release that they had found a flying saucer that turned out to be a weather balloon, what would you do to this individual? Let him spend the rest of his career in Antarctica or maybe as the supervisor of an Air Force scrap yard? Then, you have to remember he is the commander of the 509th Bomb Wing, the only nuclear-capable organization in the world at the time. This is utter incompetence! And when you look at it further, the fact that if he actually thought the material that was later photographed in general Ramey's office was part of an extraterrestrial spaceship, you would need to question the man's intelligence or sanity. The man in charge of the Roswell Army Airfield can't tell the difference between a weather balloon and a spacecraft? This is what a military man would consider as a defining moment. One that their incompetence would end their career, or their genius would catapult their success.

To be fair, anyone reviewing this situation needs to consider the months leading up to the press release. There had been hundreds of UFO reports and what were being described as flying discs in the United States. Is it possible that the officers of the RAAF honestly believed this debris was from what people were describing as a flying disc, and equating the sightings to a type of military craft or weather balloon?

It just makes a person wonder, especially when the man who publicly released such controversial and inaccurate information was ultimately promoted to four-star general and on February 19, 1965, was assigned as vice chief of staff of the United States Air Force. This is the second-highest ranking position in the Air Force. You would not and cannot attain such lofty rank and assignments with such incredible responsibility after misidentifying a weather balloon for a flying saucer.

Through the years, there have been beliefs and accusations

that Lt. Haut took it upon himself to write and disseminate the famous Roswell press release. I find this position troublesome for the mere fact that anything made public out of a governmental office, especially one that contains secrets relating to national security, would have to be approved by the chain of command. Even though it is reported that Haut and Blanchard were close friends, it would have reflected irresponsibly on Blanchard's part to allow his low-ranking PIO to write and release anything he wished. Haut was later reported to have said he received two phone calls from Washington, shutting him up, yet no mention of any corrective actions from his commanding officer.

Near Foster Ranch

But when questioning Blanchard's intent, you must examine the original press release he approved and that was drafted by Lt. Walter Haut, the 509th public information officer, for publication on July 8, 1947. When disseminated, this press release would be considered Colonel Blanchard's own words:

RAAF PRESS RELEASE

The many rumors regarding **the flying disc** became a reality yesterday when the intelligence office of the 509th Bomb Group of the Eighth Air Force, Roswell Army Airfield, was fortunate enough to **gain possession of a disc** through the cooperation of one of the local ranchers and the sheriff's office of Chaves County.

The **flying object landed** on a ranch near Roswell sometime last week. Not having phone facilities, **the rancher stored the disc** until such time as he was able to contact the sheriff's office, who in turn notified Maj. Jesse A. Marcel of the 509th Bomb Group Intelligence Office. Action was immediately taken and **the disc was picked up** at the rancher's home. It **was inspected at the Roswell Army Airfield** and subsequently loaned by Major Marcel to higher headquarters.

Later, the *Roswell Daily Record* newspaper redrafted the story to include additional information gathered from law enforcement officials and other citizens and headlined the story changing the description of the "disc" to a "saucer":

RAAF Captures **Flying Saucer** on Ranch in Roswell Region

Painfully obvious is the so-called gentrification of the word disc to saucer. Apparently, "saucer" was more appealing to the masses—somehow more interesting or respectable. One could argue they could be considered synonyms; however, this proves the inaccuracy of reporting when a news outlet wants to increase sales. Here is the actual article from the *Roswell Daily Record* dated July 8, 1947:

ROSWELL DAILY RECORD ARTICLE

The intelligence office of the 509th Bombardment group at Roswell Army Airfield announced at noon today, that the field has come into possession of a flying saucer.

According to information released by the department, over authority of Maj. J. A. Marcel, intelligence officer, the disk was recovered on a ranch in the Roswell vicinity, after an unidentified rancher had notified Sheriff Geo. Wilcox here, that he had found the instrument on his premises.

Major Marcel and a detail from his department went to the ranch and recovered the disk, it was stated.

After the intelligence officer here had inspected the instrument it was flown to higher headquarters.

The intelligence office stated that no details of the saucer's construction or its appearance had been revealed.

Mr. and Mrs. Dan Wilmot apparently were the only persons in Roswell who saw what they thought was a flying disk.

They were sitting on their porch at 105 South Penn. last Wednesday night at about ten o'clock when a large glowing object zoomed out of the sky from the southeast, going in a northwesterly direction at a high rate of speed.

Wilmot called Mrs. Wilmot's attention to it and both ran down into the yard to watch. It was in sight less than a minute, perhaps 40 or 50 seconds, Wilmot estimated.

Wilmot said that it appeared to him to be about 1,500 feet high and going fast. He estimated between 400 and 500 miles per hour.

In appearance it looked oval in shape like two inverted saucers, faced mouth to mouth, or like two old type washbowls placed together in the same fashion. The entire body glowed as though light were showing through from inside, though not like it would be if a light were underneath.

From where he stood Wilmot said that the object looked to

be about five feet in size, and making allowance for the distance it was from town he figured that it must have been fifteen to twenty feet in diameter, though this was just a guess.

Wilmot said that he heard no sound but that Mrs. Wilmot said she heard a swishing sound for a very short time.

The object came into view from the southeast and disappeared over the treetops in the general vicinity of six mile hill.

Wilmot, who is one of the most respected and reliable citizens in town, kept the story to himself hoping that someone else would come out and tell about having seen one, but finally today decided that he would go ahead and tell about it. The announcement that the RAAF was in possession of one came only a few minutes after he decided to release the details of what he had seen.

Roswell Daily Record
July 8, 1947

In a considerably simplistic forensic examination of the outlined Haut/Blanchard press release, I have indicated five sets of words that are completely contradictory to the following day's newspaper retraction by General Roger Ramey:

1. "... the flying disk..." The object located was not described as a flying saucer in the official release. This change is not a smoking gun, however, but something that should be remembered and considered when rendering judgment on the credibility of the *Roswell Daily Record* article.
2. "... gain possession of a disc..." This is a very straightforward sentence and indicates the RAAF obtained an intact disc, not scattered debris. If Blanchard were truly referring to "something" that was found in the desert, it would be incredibly

irresponsible for him to describe it generically and whole. I do not believe, in 1947 an Army airfield commander would describe wreckage as an intact disk.

3. "The flying object landed..." By all descriptions given by Major Marcel, Captain Cavitt, and later by Mack Brazel, the debris was scattered or strewn across a large area. However, by Blanchard saying "The flying object landed..." he is indicating a controlled descent to a final resting place, not scattered. Blanchard was a pilot; if he were describing an event, he would use the vernacular of a pilot. An aircraft that crashes has "crashed." An aircraft landing in the water has "ditched." An aircraft that lands has "landed."

4. "... the rancher stored the disc..." This is also a very descriptive passage indicating that the rancher, Mack Brazel, relayed to RAAF officials that he took possession of the disc for safekeeping. Not that he collected some wreckage or material, but the disc itself.

5. "... the disc was picked up..." Not material was picked up. Not debris picked up. Not parts were picked up. Blanchard is actually describing an intact disc.

6. "... it was inspected at the Roswell Army Airfield..." This sentence could be describing many different things, but it infers that RAAF officials inspected it and agreed it was a disc, not debris. Due to a lack of records, one can only assume Blanchard viewed the disc himself. Either that, or he trusted his staff enough to take their description as gospel and release the information to the public.

The root of my above assess-
ment is either (1) officials of the
RAAF had in their possession an
intact disc, or (2) Colonel William
Blanchard released a very inaccurate and sloppy version of the
actions taken and material recovered from the Foster Ranch, or
possibly (3) Blanchard and/or his
superiors formulated the press
release to further confuse the situation, thus effectively covering for
what had actually occurred.

General Roger Ramey

Whatever Colonel Blanchard effectively covered up or
orchestrated at Roswell, along with his WWII wartime and
peacetime accomplishments, impressed his superiors to such a
degree he later earned the status of second in charge of the
entire US Air Force.

Based on the little documentation we have to go on along
with informed speculation, it is evident that Colonel William
Blanchard was a co-conspirator and perpetrator in concealing
information sought out by the public and news sources relating
to the Roswell Incident. His involvement assisted in affectively
burying the events leading up to the recovery of debris or disc
and the identification of material that some believed to be of
extraterrestrial in origin.

And he used Lt. Walter Haut as the conduit with which to
spread the confusion.

5

RESPONSIBILITY AND LIEUTENANT WALTER HAUT

FORMER PUBLIC INFORMATION OFFICER 509TH BOMB GROUP ROSWELL ARMY AIRFIELD

Lieutenant Walter Haut

LIEUTENANT WALTER HAUT WAS ANYTHING BUT YOUR modern-day public information officer. He was not some administrative clerk-typist who spent his entire career behind a desk, answering media questions, coordinating public events, and organizing photo ops. He was a WWII combat aircraft bombardier who flew in many missions in the Pacific Theater in support of defeating the aggressions of the Japanese Empire. In

47

1946, like many of the other members of the 509th, he also participated in the atomic bomb test Operation Crossroads at Bikini Atoll. His job was to strategically drop devices in and around the actual atomic blast in order to collect scientific data from the explosion.

Haut's assignment as the public information officer for the 509th was outside of his normal operational skill set. It was a specialty position and one that he was specifically entrusted to by Colonel Blanchard. The PIO position would be one that may, from time to time, be entrusted with sensitive and possibly secret information.

However, something the civilian population does not always understand, you may have a top-secret clearance, but you are not authorized to access everything top secret. There must be a legitimate "need to know" for you to have such access. Oftentimes, even base commanders may not know everything that is going on within their operation, and in some cases, secret information requires dual access. This means that it requires two personnel with the same clearance and authorization to access the information together. The requirement lessens the likelihood of treasonous activity or conspiracy.

However, such clearance measures were not strictly enforced until the late 1980s, when retired US Navy warrant officer John Walker was arrested and later convicted of spying for the Soviet Union. His espionage ring consisted of a close friend, his brother, and his son, Michael Walker. Michael was a sailor assigned as a clerk with access to classified information from the combat direction center (CDC) of the nuclear aircraft carrier USS *Nimitz* (CVN-68). Michael Walker had been assigned to destroy classified documents, which he was either not doing or copying and forwarding them on for the Soviets.

Michael Walker was later convicted and sentenced to prison, for which he served fifteen years, and was released in February of 2000. His conviction actually had a ripple effect in the intelligence world and spurred changes in the way classified material is handled—at least in theory. His case was particularly impactful for me because I was assigned to *Nimitz* CDC between 1991 and 1994. Of which, I was assigned to review and disseminate secret operational information and teletype traffic and also supervised the physical destruction of the same.

Even during my tenure on *Nimitz*, there were still serious breaches of security protocol and gaps in which such materials could be compromised. And that was before email, internet, and cell phones. Imagine the security challenges of today...

For PIO Lt. Walter Haut, most classified information he would be privy to would be word of mouth. Someone actually speaking directly to him or over a secured phone system. In 1947 there were few mediums that would have preserved specific communication other than handwriting, typewriter, teletype, or telegraph. While the electronic transistor was under development and television was under experimentation in 1947, most forms of communication ceased to exist immediately after use—vanished as if the communication never occurred. This was almost certainly the case with most of Lt. Haut's assignments. Therefore, most of the information obtained from Walter Haut was through random statements to friends and family, audio and video recorded interviews conducted by ufologists, typed affidavits formatted by ufologists, and information provided to the public through open forums and at the Roswell International UFO Museum and Research Center. In his initial 1993 affidavit, Haut provided little information and indicated he had no involvement in the recovery and never saw the material. In his 1993 affidavit he had stated:

> "I believe Col. Blanchard saw the material, because he sounded positive about what the material was. There is no chance that he would have mistaken it for a weather balloon.

Neither is their [*sic*] any chance that Major Marcel would have been mistaken."

IN THE YEARS after Stanton Friedman was attributed to resurrecting the Roswell Incident, Walter Haut became one of the most interviewed witnesses to the event. Over the next two decades, Haut's recollection of the event evolved. Initially, he had few details of the event, only admitting to writing the press release. However, by his death, things changed drastically.

Upon his death, Haut gave instructions to release his final affidavit. In it, he claimed General Ramey had flown into RAAF to decide what actions to take, that Blanchard had taken him to a hangar to view the captured saucer and crew (extraterrestrials), and he claimed he actually handled the material. In one of the best books ever written on the topic of UFOs and conspiracies, in *Witness to Roswell* by Tom Carey and Don Schmitt, the authors outline Haut's detailed and concerning account of his experience related to the reported crash and recovery:

> "... Col. Blanchard took me personally to Building 84, ... I observed that it was under heavy guard both outside and inside. Once inside, I was permitted from a safe distance to first observe the object just recovered north of town. It was approx. 12-15 feet in length, not quite as wide, about 5 feet high and more of an egg shape."

His next words change everything. And if he was speaking facts, it changes our world:

> "... from a distance, I was able to see a couple of bodies under a canvas tarpaulin. Only the heads extended beyond the covering and I was not able to make out any features. The

heads did appear larger than normal and the contour of the canvas over the bodies suggested the size of a 10-year-old child."

One can only speculate what motivated Haut's lifetime of silence and his final confession after death. Was he afraid of telling the truth in fear of Air Force or government reprisals? If so, would his family be in danger even though he was now safe (if you consider dead safe...). Was it that he did not want the ridicule he would surely receive had he reported seeing little dead alien corpses under tarps? I guess it could have been all these things, and many other things as well.

I suppose we will never know for sure.

It is understandable that a man in Haut's position would initially minimize his knowledge of an above top-secret incident and attempt to avoid attracting attention. However, once the information was out in the open and there appeared to be no ramifications from the government, those involved would naturally be less guarded. And this would provide a perfect environment for those looking to share stories of their military service experience. Especially involving something as controversial as a spaceship with aliens.

It is unfortunate, however, Haut's growing story brought in skeptics and cynics who promptly dissected his claimed involvement. As a former criminal detective, I know one indication of deception is to recognize when your interviewee changes his or her story. When they make adjustments to the timeline, persons involved, and add minor details. However, on the other side, you can also resurrect details of a past event and clarify specific details that initially seemed vague or confusing.

Many skeptics have focused on the differences between his initial oral interview and the later attained written affidavits obtained by Karl Pflock in his book *Roswell in Perspective* and Tom Carey and Don Schmidt in their book *Witness to Roswell*.

In the Karl Pflock affidavit, Walter Haut confirmed several facts already known to Roswell investigators:

1. As an Army lieutenant in 1947 he was assigned as the RAAF public information officer and was notified on July 8 by the base commander Col. William Blanchard that he was in possession of a "flying saucer or parts thereof."

2. He confirmed it came from a ranch northwest of Roswell.

3. He confirmed Intelligence Officer Maj. Jesse Marcel was going to fly it to Fort Worth.

4. He wrote a press release for newspapers the *Roswell Daily Record* and *Morning Dispatch*, along with the two local radio stations, KGFL and KSWS.

5. He confirmed that Gen. Ramey reported that the material was a weather balloon.

6. He confirmed there would be no way Col. Blanchard and Maj. Marcel would misidentify weather balloon material.

7. He confirmed that Maj. Marcel said the material in the Ramey photographs was not the same material he had brought to Fort Worth.

8. Lt. Walter Haut confirms that he believes what was recovered was a "craft from outer space."

It is truly unfortunate that Karl Pflock did not obtain more details for what has maintained such a controversial position. His interview is extremely basic and simplistic. Just the who, what, when, where, and possibly why seems quite amateurish given the complexity of the claim and the age of the information. In dealing with such provocative information, investigators are required to not only get the meat and potatoes of what the interviewee asserts, but what they are concealing as well.

For me, there is a glaring error in Walter Haut's affidavit that some would passively dismiss. Reflecting on a statement analysis model and knowing both Karl Pflock and Walter Haut either had in their possession or at least easy access to, was the original press release completed by Walter Haut, one must examine his word usage. In the release, he specifically referred to the item recovered as a "flying disk" not a "flying saucer" as he described in the affidavit. This may seem insignificant, and some would say disk and saucer are synonyms. However, knowing the dispute between reported "flying disks" and the newspaper-contrived "flying saucers," there is a definite inconsistency that Pflock should have picked up on, explored and clarified.

In many cases, the person being interviewed may not be intentionally deceptive; therefore stealth and strategy should be used by the questioner. The stealth should mask any overt accusation of lying, and the strategy should be intended to reveal information relevant to the investigation that the person being questioned is not even aware of. Cognitive interviewing, using assumptive questioning, employing approaches such as the Reid Technique and, in some cases, the use of deception on the part of the investigator can be helpful. This deception is not specifically intended to trick the interviewee, it is designed to ferret out any inconsistencies, clarify positions, and hide any questioning information that would influence the answers of the person being interviewed.

In the Tom Carey and Don Schmidt 2002 affidavit published in 2007, Walter Haut confirmed everything he had originally said but added shocking details to the story not revealed in the Pflock statement.

1. Walter Haut says he received information about "remains of a downed vehicle."

2. He stated later in the day, additional civilians reported a second site north of Roswell.

3. He stated during a morning staff meeting, Gen. Ramey and Col. DuBose were in Roswell and in attendance on July 8.

4. He stated wreckage was passed around, and no one was able to identify it.

5. He stated Ramey devised a plan to divert attention from the site north of town (presumably to Marcel and Cavitt activities at the Foster Ranch).

6. He stated Blanchard dictated the "flying disk" press release to him.

7. He stated Blanchard personally took him to Building 84 (Hangar P-2) when he viewed a fifteen-foot-long egg-shaped object that had been recovered.

8. He stated he witnessed a couple of bodies presumably from the crash, and Blanchard later indicated they were about four feet tall.

9. He stated Marcel was upset about the photo operation with the parts of a weather balloon.

10. He stated he recovered some debris from one of the sites and had it on display in his office.

11. He stated he is convinced the craft and crew were from outer space.

With criminal cases, guilty suspects will often lie in order to try to get out of an arrest or conviction. In most cases, when this occurs and the investigator is aware of the deception, they will take measures to address the suspect's inconsistencies. In some cases, the suspect lies so often about so many topics of discussion there is little confirmable information provided to know exactly what had actually occurred. In such cases, investigators must rely on circumstantial and physical evidence. At face value, this is the case with Walter Haut. By changing his story and gradually providing more and more information after each preceding interview, a reasonable person would begin to doubt the validity of his testimony.

Another consideration when someone is suspected of being untruthful is their motivation. Why are they providing deceptive answers? To persecute someone else, to get themselves or someone out of trouble, to obtain power or recognition, to avoid embarrassment, to maintain their privacy, or maybe for financial gain?

Oddly enough, in 1991, Walter Haut, Glenn Dennis, and Max Littell founded a nonprofit corporation in the city of Roswell. Later in 1992, they opened the International UFO Museum and Research Center. Their goal declaration was simple: To educate, not convince, the public about the Roswell Incident and other UFO phenomenon. While the center got off to a slow start, by the end of 2016 the museum had recorded over 200,000 visitors that year, and the city added up over 248,000 hotel bookings in the area relating to visitors of the museum. In 2017, Roswell city officials estimated the seventieth anniversary would bring in $6 million during the four-day event. For a town like Roswell, which is not necessarily known for its tourism, this brings a huge infusion of money into the local economy.

Many of the Roswell Incident detractors have pointed fingers to the fact that in order for the museum to gain momentum and remain successful, more stories were needed and the more elaborate, the better. Therefore, cynics attest officials at the museum, independent investigators, and book authors supporting the UFO story failed to professionally qualify many of the key eyewitnesses. Some of whom swore to stories that later came back as a mistake of fact, situations that the witness was unable to corroborate, or exposed blatant contrived testimony and sometimes evidence.

Walter Haut's final declaration came after his death in the form of a final written statement. It is here that Mr. Haut adds to and concludes his chapter in the Roswell Incident. While some would argue that this is only a further indication of a continued deception perpetrated by him, the three questions remain: (1) is he telling the truth, (2) did he jump on the Stanton Friedman bandwagon simply to collect tourist dollars, or (3) is he continuing the deception due to his dedication to the US or at the government's direction.

Haut's final affidavit—his deathbed confession—is filled with mystery, conspiracy, and intrigue. Was his growing list of occurrences due to his improving memory or false memories brought about by well-known additional witness tales of Roswell? Were the additions to his story based on facts as he remembers them or contrived explanations of what seemed in his mind to make sense? As an old WWII bombardier, did he want to drop one final big one on the Roswell Incident and bust open the entire government cover-up or just to continue the ruse? The truth of the matter is, until the government rolls out an egg-shaped spacecraft and some four-foot-tall alien bodies, we will never know.

Ultimately, no matter what we may think, Walter Haut was part of the greatest generation this country will ever see. Did he partake in the original crash cover-up? Maybe. Did he continue to facilitate conspiracies of the event? Yes. But whatever the case, he not only served America honorably, but he also served the city of Roswell and is one of Roswell's finest citizens.

[6]

THE BOY WITNESS JESSE MARCEL JR.

SON OF MAJOR JESSE MARCEL

Left: Jesse Marcel, Jr., Right: Author, Greg Lawson

IN THE FALL OF 1969, I STOOD AT THE SIDE OF MY YARD, waiting—something I was not used to as a five-year-old boy. I had not yet mastered the art of patience (something I am still working on fifty years later). You see, my next-door neighbor was a pilot. And not just any pilot, he was an Air Force major who flew F-4 Phantoms—my favorite. But I stood and waited, dressed in the mini–Air Force officer's uniform my mother had bought for me at Bergstrom Air Force Base in Austin, Texas.

Earlier that year, during what was known as Agua Fest in Austin, my family had ventured out to the base where the Air Force Tactical Air Command had an airshow and static display. That was my first real involvement around the military, and it was a transformational experience. I remember seeing all kinds of aircraft and one in particular that I could not believe would actually fly. I believe it was a C-5 cargo plane, which could practically transport our house inside it. I was amazed. Later we visited the vendor area, and that was where my mother bought my uniform.

After what seemed an eternity, the major finally drove up and parked in his driveway. When he got out of his car, I saluted him. I remember he came over, and we talked, but I don't remember about what. He inspected my uniform and adjusted my collar. After several minutes, he saluted me back and retired into his house. I remember he was a kind man and, on that day, made a little boy feel special. Several years later my mother heard that he was shot down in Vietnam and spent some time in the Hanoi Hilton but was a returned POW at the end of the war.

These events were probably the things that initially got me interested in keeping an eye on the sky, flying, and my interest in space travel. Those things and comic books such as DC's *Weird War Tales*, Space Ranger, and *Tales of the Unexplained*. I'm sure they kept my imagination busy also. However, it was the things that I would see in the skies in 1969 to 1970 that solidified my suspicions.

From time to time at my home in north Austin, I watched large silver disks as they trekked across, high in the sky. Fortunately for me, I had the major next door, and I was not afraid to ask him questions. One day, late in the afternoon, the major was mowing his lawn, and I saw one. A large disk-shaped object, extremely high in the air, moving steadily across the sky. I waved and got the major's attention. I pointed to the object, and we talked about it. It was then he explained that depending on the direction of the wind, weather balloons that were launched from Bergstrom Air Force Base would come over our neighborhood. Particularly, he pointed out these balloons become excessively big when they get high into the air and, depending on their payload, flatten out some. He said that early in the evening or morning, when the Sun is extremely low, the light from the Sun can reflect and make the object look like a shiny coin. He pointed up and said, "Just like that one."

While I remained interested in the sky, I can say from that point on, shiny objects in the heavens were significantly less interesting to me. While I remained interested in the NASA moon missions and over the years watched the progress and development of the NASA Shuttle Program, my aspirations waned and the reality set in that I was probably never going to become and astronaut or any kind of space traveler for that matter. However, later in life, because of my passion for space travel, I was accepted as a Solar System Ambassador for NASA's Jet Propulsion Laboratory, speaking on behalf of NASA at institutions of learning and community events.

For years, my interest in space travel drifted. It wasn't until 1984, while stationed with the US Army in Alaska, that I saw my first satellite. And then came that fateful day in September of 1989 when I sat down in my little apartment in Austin and watched the now famous episode of *Unsolved Mysteries*, season 2, episode 1, the Roswell Incident. My interest in space travel was piqued again. Oddly enough, within a year, I was enlisted as an operations specialist in the US Navy and serving on board the aircraft carrier USS *Nimitz* (CVN-68). Serving in the Air Detection and Tracking module, Surface Warfare module, as the Fleet Communications petty officer in the Combat Direction Center, and as a Joint Operations Tactical Systems database manager, the things I saw as an operations specialist solidified my unwavering belief that there are some things flying in our skies that we cannot, at this time, explain.

After my service with the Navy, I maintained my interest in space travel and desired to stay current with future technologies and trends pertaining to aerial phenomena. But it wasn't until 2005 that I seriously turned my interest to Roswell and the events that occurred there in 1947.

I believe it was 2007 when I was fortunate enough to be helping set up a vendor table for the UFO Festival in the Roswell civic center. It was there I first met Jesse Marcel Jr. He was at the very next table, and I introduced myself as an enthusiast of the Roswell Incident and as a professional criminal investigator. By that time, I had about fifteen years of civilian law enforcement experience and was working as a detective for a large agency in Texas. We chatted for several minutes, and without asking, he privately described to me his role in the Roswell story. From my investigative experience, I realized Jesse Marcel Jr. was not trying to convince me of the events he experienced in 1947, he was merely telling me what had happened the night his father brought home the material he had collected from the Foster Ranch. Material that his father described as "... not of this Earth..."

You see, I point this out because there are certain ways people go about telling you a story. Oftentimes they concentrate on what's important to them and try to narrow you down to specific details that would prove the incident to be true. Oftentimes after they tell the story, if the tale seemed plausible to them and sounded good to them, they will lean back slightly and display a smile of gratification. Much like saying, "Yeah, I bet he believes that." Or they may qualify themselves by saying something like, you know I was raised as a Christian, and then go on with their story. Or at the end of the story, specifically ask, "You believe me, don't you?"

Jesse Marcel Jr. did none of that.

Somewhere along the conversation, he pointed out he was currently writing a book about the Roswell Incident and was thinking of self-publishing. I had previously self-published a novel, and finding common ground, we continued brainstorming each other's ideas throughout the day. It was a great experience for me, not only because Jesse Jr. was such a humble and kind man, but because he may have been the only living human being I knew who had actually touched material from a spacecraft operated by an alien species.

During the next several years, I saw Jesse Jr. annually at the Roswell UFO Festival. And every year we just started where we had left off. There was something about the man that was genuine. So honest. So trustworthy, that it gave additional credence to what he was saying. What he was reporting to the world.

In every vocation, every profession, every occupation, there are unique skill sets. While portions of these skills may partially bleed over to the others, specific skills are engrained and refined to the point that surpass the familiar knowledge gleaned from the bleed over. As far as investigative procedures, anyone can learn to obtain the who, what, when, where, how, and sometimes the why. But the ability to question persons in such a way as to not lead their answers, and the ability to recognize subtle signs of deception cannot come out of watching a TV show or reading a book. It comes from receiving formal education from qualified instructors, collectively learning from years of experience, and being able to implement the industry's best policies and practices.

Jesse Jr. could have easily fabricated something more out of this world than what he admitted his father showed him late that night of the recovery. He could have bolstered his story with additional details. He could have described the debris in a more fanciful way to make the tale more interesting.

And to make him money.

But he didn't.

Jesse Jr. stuck to his story. The details he shared were minimal. The circumstances were not grandiose. The amount of the debris not substantial. He gave his account from the memory of his eleven-year-old mind and described a normal night when his father came home, woke him up, and showed him and his mom the material. Jesse Jr. insisted that it seemed special at the time; however, after burying the secret, the impact of his memory also faded.

A day before Jesse Sr. was inducted in the Roswell Hall of Fame, Jesse Jr. and I chatted about this distinction. He was always very modest about his role in the Roswell Incident. However, he understood that his testimony, the fact of his father bringing the material home lent credibility to his father's story. This was huge in a time where many UFO investigators and Roswell debunkers were trying to discredit his father, the former Maj. Jesse Marcel, by catching him making any untruthful or inconsistent remarks—and there were some. There are only really three questions an investigator must ask of untruthfulness: (1) is it a mistake of fact or memory, (2) is it a lie of omission, or (3) is it a lie of commission?

Over the course of decades, many investigators searched government and private records for statements he made to friends and family, interviews he did with newspapers and magazines, and interviews he had on TV and radio. Many of these debunkers had brought into question several of the military, educational, and training claims Marcel Sr. had made over the years. Make no mistake, these attempts were intended to be used to discredit his testimony and in theory proving what Marcel said could not be trusted. It was used to weaken any of his claims. The problem with that logic is it is a character attack —not an attack on his assertions or any overt facts. This tactic, known as an ad hominem (against the man), is designed to distract observers away from the truth of the matter and provide a false trail to pursue against the character of the person. While character is obviously important, they can still tell the truth as well.

As a career criminal investigator trained in interview techniques, interrogation techniques, and cross-examination techniques, I know and understand that just because someone fabricates or fails at correct memory recall decades after their involvement in an event does not mean what they are telling you didn't happen. It certainly does not help if your key eyewitness gets people, places, things, times, and dates wrong; however, it does not mean the event did not happen.

I have read articles, watched TV programs, and observed panel discussions where the participants, expert witnesses, and pundits get completely embattled about specific locations, times, and dates. While these elements can be extremely important when it comes to qualifying your witness or exculpating a possible suspect, investigators must stay focused on the core events in the incident. For instance, in some cases criminal warrants are obtained using a detailed description of the suspect instead of the person's specific name; the investigators know several specifics about the person such as tattoos, place of employment, or other unique characteristics. In many cases the time and date on the affidavit of a person charged with a crime may read: *On or about July 4, 1947,* or *Sometime between July 2 and July 6, 1947.* Just because you do not have the time and dates exactly correct does not mean the event did not happen.

I have interviewed murder suspects for hours, and the whole time I was getting multiple indications of classic deceptions. From body posturing, verbal distraction, and too much or lack of eye contact, I have accused these persons of committing a crime. Only to later realize they had nothing to do with it—the cues of deception I was observing did not originate because they were trying to cover up the crime I was investigating—they were trying to cover up other crimes or embarrassments they were afraid I would uncover within the course of my investigation. Drug possession or use and sexual infidelity can often manifest itself as deception when a person is interviewed on a completely different topic.

Gleaning truthful and accurate information from a victim, witness, or suspect is a complicated endeavor and one that is very perishable. Going off of body language alone is misleading, the evaluation of mere verbal behavior patterns can be ambiguous, and the reliance on eye movements as a deception indicator is too simplistic. It is all of these and many other things in the course of interviewing your subject that will lead you to the truth.

Due to my education, training, and experience, I unequivocally assert Jesse Marcel Jr. told the truth, the whole truth, and nothing but the truth. He was a humble servant of his family, community, country, and to the Roswell legacy.

He was an eyewitness to a portion of the event.

[7]
DOING THE RIGHT THING WITH WILLIAM WARE "MACK" BRAZEL

RANCH FORMAN, FOSTER RANCH, CORONA, NEW MEXICO

William Ware "Mack" Brazel

HERE IS WHERE THE MYSTERY ACTUALLY BEGINS...

Or does it?

In the previous months leading up to the Roswell Incident, there had been scores of reported UFO sightings throughout the United States. One of the most notable was that of Kenneth Arnold. To his death Kenneth passionately believed that what he saw that day was not of this Earth. In an April 1949 *Saturday Evening Post* interview, Kenneth was quoted:

> "... There is no doubt in my mind but what these objects are aircraft of a strange design, and material that is unknown to the civilization of this earth."(Shalett).

Kenneth's report and the reports from many other American citizens fueled a UFO craze during 1947. The fascination of intercepting and identifying one of these reported "flying disks" led to additional pressure on the Air Force, and in some cases, rewards were offered for a flying disk or materials from a flying disk. Because at this point, and to this day for that matter, no one really knew or knows what these flying disks were.

In addition, rewards for balloon material were something well known around the Roswell region. In some cases, reward tags were attached to the balloon payloads, requesting that if the equipment was found, it should be returned to the owner, the Air Force, other government entities, etc. As far as rewards went, the amount of the reward was based on the fiscal value or intellectual value of the material recovered.

Depending on the version of the *Roswell Daily Record* you choose to believe, before or after Army Air Forces personnel got to Mack Brazel, it is not debated that he located a debris field on the Foster Ranch that contained what appeared to be wreckage made of strange foil-like material, thin structural supports, and strips of a rubberlike substance.

Years later, Mack's neighbor Loretta Proctor was interviewed by multiple Roswell investigators and always maintained her story. She told how Mack had come to her house and showed her and her husband, Floyd, a fragment of the material he had gathered from the crash site. She and Floyd guessed it was part of one of the flying disks that had been seen and reported by so many people. According to her, they encouraged

Mack to turn it in to authorities for a possible reward. Afterwards, Loretta swore Mack was kept by the Army for possibly a week, and once he was released, he never spoke of it again.

Unfortunately, Loretta was the only person still alive when the Roswell investigators came to interview her, and none of her story can be substantiated. But her story is not too hard to believe. Given the circumstances and his knowledge of the material he found, it is plausible the government did detain Mack due to concerns about national security. This occurred just after WWII and in the beginnings of the Cold War. It would be plausible if Mack had obtained additional information about the material found, whether it was top-secret MOGUL balloon and surveillance equipment or a ship from outer space, authorities might have wanted to conduct a comprehensive debriefing of Mack's background, affiliations, and what he knew.

It is unfortunate that both Mack and his wife, Maggie, died before the Roswell Incident was exposed by Friedman. There are no official interviews or statements from either of them to provide any clarity to the situation. However, in every interview collected from anyone who knew Brazel, he was described as a salt-of-the-earth kind of guy. Loyal, trustworthy, and honest. A true man's man. He was working as the foreman for the J. B. Foster Ranch located about thirty miles southeast of Corona. In an interview he gave to the *Roswell Daily Record* on July 9, 1947, he described the circumstances and what he had found on the ranch that led up to the RAAF's press release of a "flying saucer." Oddly enough, Mack's story did not exactly match what had been reported by the RAAF, and many believe intelligence or counterintelligence officials of the RAAF debriefed him on the seriousness of his findings and constructed a narrative for him to later follow. This would explain why there were discrepancies in the first article written in the *Roswell Daily Record* on July 8 generated from the Lt. Walter Haut RAAF press release. The release indicated Brazel collected the material within the last week, and in Brazel's subsequent in-person interview for the July 9 edition, he reported collecting the material on June 14.

When Brazel came across the debris scattered in the desert, he was intrigued by it. He wondered if this was one of the reported "flying disks" that had been seen by so many people. Like so many other things in a cold case, dates are often gleaned from pure speculation. The discovery to his first report timeline would span somewhere between June 14, 1947, and July 6, 1947. Obviously, if any human being would come across an unrecognizable, supposed space vehicle, you would think they would immediately report it to the authorities. However, this was not the case here. If the June 14 timeline is accurate, that would indicate Brazel did not think the material was that strange or important enough to immediately collect it or report it to the authorities. Whether it was because whatever he found did not elicit an immediate reaction from Brazel or the fact that the J. B. Foster Ranch was so remote his reporting was delayed, the truth remains that Brazel did not immediately and directly inform officials. This remains true whether his notification was three weeks delayed or three days delayed.

The date disparity from the two *Roswell Daily Record* articles is a fact that many skeptics use to try to bolster their assertion that this was nothing more than a weather balloon. However, it is a fact that Brazel had found weather balloons in the past, and he knew what they were. What he found this time was a mystery to him.

Whether Brazel found the wreckage on June 14 or July 4, the bottom line is we know on July 7, 1947, he went into Roswell and visited Chavez County Sheriff George Wilcox and reported that he had found debris on the ranch that may be from a "flying disk." Wilcox, not knowing anything about the material, decided to notify the RAAF and was put in touch with Major Jesse Marcel, the head of intelligence at the 509th.

According to Brazel's official statement to the *Roswell Daily Record* July 9 edition, after speaking with Sheriff Wilcox on July 6, he escorted Major Marcel and "a man in plain clothes," later identified as counterintelligence officer Captain Sheridan Cavitt, to the Foster Ranch, where they stayed the night in the ranch house, also known as the Hines House. The next day Brazel took them to the impact area, which he depicted as approximately two hundred yards in diameter. There on July 7, they collected the remaining debris and compiled it back at the Hines House. Brazel would later describe it as tinfoil, paper, tape, rubber, and sticks. He said they tried to piece it back together; however, they were unable to.

At the end of the article, Brazel says something very curious:

"… but if I find anything else, besides a bomb they are going to have a hard time getting me to say anything about it."
    Roswell Daily Record

This is a very curious statement and one that ufologists and debunkers have battled over for years. Some investigators believe that from the time the RAAF became involved and Brazel did the interview for the July 9 edition, he was thoroughly debriefed on the secrecy of the material, and he was given orders within the interest of national security to downplay the materials found and the events that transpired.

Some believe after the men collected the material, they returned to Roswell with Brazel, where he was detained for several days—there is abundant witness testimony gathered by Carey, Schmitt, and others to support this premise. This would explain Brazel being back in town on July 8 for the interview. But once again, in a thirty-one-plus-year-old investigation, nailing down specific times and dates is extremely difficult.

What we do know is that while in the custody of government officials from the RAAF, something happened. Something changed the way this honest and hardworking cowboy viewed members of the Army Air Forces to the point that he no longer trusted them.

While conducting forensic statement analysis, evaluators will look for a series of specific things. One of them is a complete change in the person's view of the circumstances. Such as a man being investigated for the death of his wife may refer to her as his wife throughout his story and change the word "wife" to her first name (let's say Jane), indicating the death occurred at that time in the story. Thereafter he calls her Jane. This often occurs subconsciously because he believes a good man like himself could never kill someone who is his wife, but he could surely kill someone like Jane. In Brazel's case, we do not have a statement from him written or spoken in his own words to analyze—we only have a doctored newspaper edition of what the reporter said he stated. And in my direct experience, news reporters more often than not add in their own suppositions to the mix—they can be a blessing and a curse to any researcher. More of a curse to any cop.

So what did Brazel mean when he said:

"... but if I find anything else, besides a bomb they are going to have a hard time getting me to say anything about it."

Was it because when he went into the sheriff's office, he wanted to be confidential about what he was reporting and it blew up into an Associated Press media sensation, embarrassing him and his family? Or was it what he had to endure at the hands of the RAAF command and counterintelligence staff?

It's hard to say for sure.

However, forty plus years later, Friedman, Carey, Schmidt, Randle, and many other investigators will end up taking many statements from former RAAF service personnel, Roswell citizens, and family members who support, unequivocally, that Mack Brazel was detained and debriefed by the military for days after his report to Sheriff Wilcox. However, this information did not come out for decades later and no one has been able to corroborate his confinement or debriefing/interrogation through any official records or personal documents from that time.

Even Brazel's son Bill had extraordinarily little information to assist in the investigation. He simply relayed to Randal and others that his father didn't speak of it. He had possibly spoken to Bill's wife, Shirley, but didn't give her all the facts either. Of Mack's other children, none ever handed over a smoking gun. His daughter, Bessie, who reportedly helped gather much of the material brought to Sheriff Wilcox, believed her father's stories about being jailed by the RAAF, but had no substantial additional details. His son Paul continued in his father's footsteps as a foreman for the Foster family in Texas and had no further input.

Oddly enough, Mack's son Vernon, the one reported being with Mack when they found the debris, was described by some ufologist to have mysteriously disappeared in the 1960s and has never been interviewed. This is apparently partially true. However, other searches by investigators track him leaving New Mexico in his late teens, and there are government records of him living in Virginia and California. According to Ancestry.com, Vernon Richard Brazel died in 1967 ("The Children Who"). And according to the book *The Children of Roswell* by Tom Carey and Don Schmitt, former neighbor Loretta Proctor reported that Vernon did not handle his experience with the incident well. Researcher Tony Bragalia was able to piece some of his story together. According to him, Loretta reported Vernon got out of New Mexico as soon as he could, served for a time with the US Navy on board USS *Hassayampa* (AO-145), and later killed himself with a gunshot to the head. In fact, Vernon not only left New Mexico, he changed his name and married a woman, never telling her who he really was.

No official statement was ever taken from Vernon.

While we assume it would be likely that Brazel participated in radio interviews about the incident, no recordings of his accounts survived. Officials of radio station KGFL in Roswell confirmed they had interviewed him, and officially, he did not stray too far from his interview given to the *Roswell Daily Record*.

In the following seven decades after Mack Brazel walked into Sheriff Wilcox's office, friends, family, and acquaintances have come forward and given testimony to dozens of reporters and investigators to the outcome of Mack's interaction with the Roswell Army Airfield. Many of these accounts are uncorroborated verbal testimony and cannot be equivalently confirmed, because of Mack's death in 1963. Several of the accounts do match up with other self-proclaimed witnesses to the RAAF handling of him, or at least his absence for several days just after he alerted the Army. Also there have been assertions that the government provided him a payment for his silence and, at the very least, allegations he received a new pickup truck to keep quiet. None of these claims have been substantiated, but that does not mean the Army Air Force did not detain him. However, it could be just as likely, due to his quiet demeanor, he was taking care of personal business.

Maybe even buying a new pickup.

Of my many trips to Roswell, I spent much time tracking little pieces of the puzzle. Little missing pieces the Roswell investigators may have overlooked. One of these was trying to locate any vehicle registration records the state of New Mexico has for Mack Brazel. Specifically, in 1947. To date I have found none. However, I have spoken with several officials from the New Mexico Motor Vehicle Division, and they have all given me different answers to the same questions. It's the DMV, what can we expect but poor service and ambiguity? But this does not indicate conspiracy on their part, more likely incompetency and not truly knowing if vehicle records from the 1940s still exists or where they are even stored. And obviously, a new pickup registered to Brazel at the time would not get us any closer to the truth; however, it would be just one more little piece of intrigue.

One must consider that it is odd Mack Brazel was the only citizen reported to be detained by the RAAF. Even in subsequent investigations thirty plus years later, no one asserted additional persons were detained. There are many who provided testimony of RAAF officials debriefing citizens and even threatening them, but none for any prolonged length of time. Even Mack's son Bill asserted in multiple interviews that his father was bitter about how the RAAF jailed him, and he had to submit to taking a head-to-toe physical examination. But once again, this information is second and thirdhand. Mack had three sons and a daughter. None of whom had firsthand knowledge of his treatment by the RAAF, only that their father was very guarded about it and did not speak of it freely. That is what makes this case and so many other cold cases almost impossible to prove—the main players are all dead.

The day that Brazel brought the material in to Sheriff George Wilcox, he spoke with Frank Joyce, a radio announcer at the local station KGFL. It was regular for Frank to inquire with the sheriff if there was anything newsworthy for the day. Joyce was allowed to interview Brazel over the phone. Unfortunately, this time, like some others, the conversation was not recorded. Of the only reported recording, it was said Brazel actually went to the KGFL owner's residence, Walt Whitmore, and spoke with him directly. Decades later, it was reported that the interview was recorded; however, it was later confiscated by personnel of the RAAF.

Once again, we have nothing.

All in all, Brazel gave a total of three radio interviews. A telephone interview with KGFL while in Sheriff Wilcox's office, a recorded interview at the KGFL radio's owner's house, Walt Whitmore, that was later reported to have been confiscated by the government, and an unrecorded interview with an El Paso radio station. We can only assume during the interviews he continued with the same account of finding the material/disk and bringing it to the sheriff's attention. Throughout the entire Roswell story, this rancher, this simple cowboy, had and maintained his credibility in the face of serious controversy. As a man and a citizen of the United States, he reported what he knew and took the rest of it to the grave with him.

It's odd for someone who valued his privacy so dearly, he became, and to this day is, the most famous ranch foreman in New Mexico history.

8

THE RELUCTANT WITNESS – GEORGE WILCOX

CHAVES COUNTY SHERIFF, ROSWELL, NEW MEXICO

George Wilcox

AFTER BEING TREATED IN A HOSPITAL SPECIALIZING IN people with mental disorders, George Wilcox, the former high sheriff of Chaves County, died. To the end, his family blamed the termination of his law enforcement career and decline of his health on the personnel of the Roswell Army Airfield. In many interviews by Roswell citizen investigators, four decades or more after the incident, family members described the action of the government subsequent to Mack Brazel notifying Wilcox of what he had found as destroying George's law enforcement career.

According to researcher James Bartley and others, George was later diagnosed with early onset of Alzheimer's disease and spent some time in what was described as a mental asylum before his death ("In Memory of"). In some reports it is inferred that his wife, Inez Wilcox, believed the military had actually injected him with a substance that caused him to have memory loss and paranoia to the point one time he actually assaulted her. This claim is unsubstantiated but follows the same line of thinking.

For four years in the late 1940s, Inez and George occupied the run-down sheriff's home quarters in the downstairs of the archaic county jail in Roswell. The structure was built around 1900, and like many other government facilities connected to criminality, it was not high on the priority list for maintenance or upgrades. The cells were tiny with no windows, and there was no accommodation of any kind for recreation. These are what modern jailers would call temporary holding cells. These kinds of horrific facilities led to rulings in case law changing the directives for the doors and windows of jails and the mandatory recreation time outdoors.

The staffing within the sheriff's office was neglected as well. Initially, the office was only funded for the sheriff, two deputies, and a jailer. However, the sheriff's office did oversee the Sheriff's Posse—a group of uniformed men and women volunteers sworn as honorary deputies who could be called on for emergencies and to provide a presence at civic functions.

During George's term in office, Inez assisted in the running of the jail, performing some maintenance duties, meal preparation, and she was also called on to accompany the movement of female prisoners and worked closely with detained juveniles. She even ran for the office when George's period had expired;

however, she was defeated. During that time, the one thing George did keep her from was any involvement with the Roswell Incident.

According to family members, Inez believed men from the government and Army Air Force personnel threatened to do harm or worse to George and his family if he were ever to talk about the incident. This assertion was made by Barbara Dugger, Inez and George's granddaughter, in an affidavit taken by Karl Pflock. She also believed George had gone to the site, viewing a large burnt area, debris, and four space beings, one of them still being alive (Pflock). None of this was documented during the time of the incident, and the information came forward after the airing of the *Unsolved Mysteries* episode on Roswell.

While speaking with Don Schmitt in the 1990s, more than forty years later, Barbara's mother, Elizabeth Tulk, provided supportive testimony to the existence of a military operation to recover a flying saucer or the debris of one in Roswell. Wilcox's other daughter, Phyllis McGuire, confirmed in an audio interview for the *UFO Crash at Roswell* audio documentary narrated by Don Schmitt that Sheriff Wilcox had dispatched two deputies (which according to records would have been his whole law enforcement staff—although they could have been from his sheriff's posse) out to the location. They reportedly witnessed a large burnt area of prairie grass.

There is a saying in law enforcement: "If you didn't document it, it didn't happen." Now we all know this is not factually true, but it is figuratively true—if one does not record or document an action or incident within a reasonable amount of time after the incident, it lessens the information's legitimacy. Documenting facts just after an incident puts the incident into context and provides a foundation to the facts as the witness or reportee knows them to be. In 2020, all law enforcement officers know this to be true. Not doing so otherwise subjects the information to be contrived and/or possibly fabricated. Thus lies the dilemma with much of the Roswell Incident—no initial docu-mentation or reporting at the time of the incident, then hearsay information from third-party witnesses three decades or more later.

The real problem rests in the lack of documentation from the sheriff's office both on the part of the sheriff and his deputies, assuming what Phillis was saying is true. Much along the thinking of Sheridan Cavitt, Sheriff Wilcox may have come to the conclusion that this was a nonevent. Just a standard weather balloon recovery that became confusing and nothing more. Or he may have taken what Elizabeth recounted and felt he and his family would be in grave danger should he document or relay the information. In most modern law enforcement agen-cies, if they are tasked with helping out military personnel or another law enforcement agency, at the bare minimum, they will write an "Assist Other Agency" report.

But that is now, not 1947.

Whatever the case, the most we know about Sheriff George Wilcox and his involvement comes from historical newspaper reports and anecdotes of those related to him through family or friendship. None of which gets us any closer to the truth. What we know for sure is based on newspaper-documented events in 1947 that Sheriff Wilcox:

1. Spoke with Brazel about what he found and felt like it was a military matter.
2. Notified Roswell Army Airfield.
3. Possibly sent out two deputies to the Foster ranch or another site.
4. Fielded phone calls from around the world that were generated from the initial *Roswell Daily Record* article.

After the 1989, *Unsolved Mysteries* episode, proclaimed

witnesses came forward and gave the details of Sheriff Wilcox receiving threats from the military and his role in being coerced into suppressing the truth of the crash at the behest of the Air Force. These were numerous.

Perhaps the most disturbing fact to come out of the sheriff's involvement in the Roswell Incident was his solitary position of being the go-between for the Roswell Army Airfield and the regular citizens of Chavez County and the world. George Wilcox was simply a conscientious man who wanted to do a good job and serve his community. He wasn't in it for the fame. He wasn't in it for the excitement. And he certainly wasn't in it for the money. His situation should teach us all a lesson—sometimes fate finds you, and you have no choice in the matter but to play the cards you are dealt.

So, in the immortal words of coach and commentator John Madden, "Don't do anything great unless you can handle the congratulations…"

George Wilcox did his best.

9

THE MASTER OBFUSCATER CAPTAIN SHERIDAN CAVITT

COUNTERINTELLIGENCE OFFICER 509TH BOMB WING

Captain Sheridan Cavitt

OF ALL THE ROSWELL INCIDENT CONSPIRATORS AND witnesses, Sheridan Cavitt certainly had the most fun with the ufologists—just look at his picture. This man had game...

Roswell Incident debunkers often rely on Cavitt's statements, misstatements, or silence and use it as a foundation for their assertions that this incident was nothing more than a balloon surveillance experiment gone wrong or right, depending on whom you ask. It is interesting how the debunkers would use a man's testimony whose entire occupation was to collect information, then confuse and derail facts in an attempt to hide the truth. Don't get me wrong, this entire situation and the subsequent forty-plus-year investigation is very confusing. That is why it is so important for those of us reviewing the material after the fact that we understand the military culture and climate of US society at the time.

While Cavitt never actually accused any of his co-workers of untruthfulness or outright lying, he did skillfully plant the seeds of doubt in the statements they did make. In an attempt to truly try to decipher this man's scattered statements and sworn testimony, we must attempt to establish what kind of man he really was. First, we need to understand the type of men who were recruited into the counterintelligence core of WWII.

In 1917 the corps of intelligence police was established by the War Department. It consisted of about fifty men with the rank of sergeant, and the entire unit was deployed to France, where they were merged with French divisional intelligence sections. These men were tasked with fraud and graft (black market) investigations along with counterespionage security concerns. After the war, these numbers dwindled, and it wasn't until the beginning of the Second World War that significant attention was paid to not only gathering intelligence but subverting espionage and treason as well.

Two months after the attack on Pearl Harbor, in February of 1942, a significant recruiting effort was formulated. The designers of a more modern intelligence unit changed its name to the counterintelligence branch of the military intelligence division. And it was truly a change in name only. The same men were in charge, recruiting in the same way. In gathering manpower, the counterintelligence corps looked for men with a high school diploma and of the highest integrity. In the coming months, the intelligence police grew to over 500, then quickly to over 1,000. At this point with so many enlisted personnel, a complement of officers was assigned to manage the units. Over the next three years, the counterintelligence corps grew to file over 500 commissioned officers and over 4,400 enlisted men. They conducted counterintelligence operations in every theater of the war. The recruiting efforts of these counterintelligence personnel would be slightly modified, influenced by the experience they gained overseas. Recruitment efforts began reaching out to a diverse group of civilians who ranged in many different occupations. This diversity seemed to help broaden their ability to understand the challenges and adapt to the environment. However, by the end of the war, the organizers of the corps recognize their number one failure as not teaching their agents the foreign language that would be used in their theater of deployment.

When the war was over, once again the United States military made efforts to downsize their personnel units, including the counterintelligence core. The corps' focus was redirected away from the axis powers and began focusing in on the spread of communism. While many counterintelligence corps personnel were assigned to investigate and prosecute war crimes committed by the leaders of Japan and Germany, others were gearing up to the new communist challenge. In doing so, they became a separate branch of the intelligence division.

These counterintelligence corps (CIC) personnel were assigned to many different theaters and to many espionage investigations. One of their biggest missions was Operation Paperclip. Counterintelligence Corps personnel and special agents were tasked with identifying, securing, and relocating over 1,600 German scientists, engineers, and technicians. These Germans were then assigned to special projects within the United States.

In 1947 Operation Paperclip was in full force.

As I said before, I don't believe most Americans can even imagine the paranoia United States citizens dealt with in 1947.

Communism spreading, the United States government bringing former Nazi scientists into the US to conduct secret experiments, foreign agents infiltrating the government, and the near unlimited authority given to special agents of the Counterintelligence Corps and other governmental entities to exercise power and suppress information from the United States citizenry.

Sheridan Cavitt was one such man.

There's no doubt that the location of the 509th Bomb Wing at the Roswell Army Airfield in Roswell, New Mexico, was no accident. This area of the country is sparse, harsh, and isolated. It would truly be difficult for any country to conduct any sort of military operation against the 509th Bomb Wing. The vast desert of central New Mexico provides little to no cover for any airborne craft or vehicle for the purpose of infiltration.

It is rare enough to be an officer in the Intelligence Corps, but to be a commissioned officer in the Counterintelligence Corps is truly a rarity. Possibly one of the smallest and most exclusive groups of officers in all the militaries. And for Captain Cavitt to be assigned to the 509th, we can assume that he was one of the best of the best. As so many Roswell investigators have said before, the 509th Bomb Wing was the only nuclear-capable delivery platform in the world at the time. Which would make it the most secure and most secretive. You would further surmise that any officer who would be assigned to the 509 would be the best of the best. However, the thing you must also understand is that some of the most important counterintelligence work was being done in Europe and Asia at this time. I know firsthand, from serving in the United States Army, United States Navy, and United States Air Force, more often than not slots are more likely filled by personnel availability than the best-qualified person.

While posting for billets will list a large number of important required qualifications, the simple fact is, typically, only the individuals slated for a new duty assignment will be selected.

That in itself is a huge limitation to the personnel you receive. I can officially say I do not know what special qualifications Captain Sheridan Cavitt possessed to obtain his position at the 509th, I just know that he too is human and prone to flaw.

Within this book, I have tried to obtain most of my research material from the time period that it occurred. That is a true challenge for the simple fact that not much of the Roswell Incident was actually documented. Cavitt is one of the few people who we can confirm was not only stationed at Roswell Army Airfield as a counterintelligence officer, we can affirm that he accompanied Major Marcel to the Foster Ranch debris site. However, most of what we know about Sheridan Cavitt we obtained from *The Roswell Report* compiled by the headquarters of United States Air Force dated 1995 and independent Roswell investigators. The report is a highly bias self-serving document that never considered the possibility of a UFO conspiracy, and the information gleaned by some of the Roswell investigators has been questionable in its context.

Because of this bias, many of the credible thirdhand witnesses were never reinterviewed by the Air Force. The document's Executive Summary, the very first page, sets the mood of the Air Force's entire investigation on the matter, beginning with:

"The 'Roswell Incident' refers to an event that supposedly happened in July, 1947, wherein the Army Air Forces (AAF) allegedly recovered remains of a crashed 'flying disc' near Roswell, New Mexico."
    The Roswell Report 1995

Let's take a look at "supposedly" and "allegedly." The fact is, what we contemporarily refer to as the "Roswell Incident" did occur on or about July 1947. And the fact is that members of the Air Force did recover remains of a crashed airborne apparatus—whether it was and extraterrestrial craft or manmade—people in the 1947 referred to such things as a "flying disk."

In fact, in the Air Force's Roswell report, the investigators and authors Colonel Richard Weaver and Lieutenant James McAndrew assert that most of the interviews and documentation gathered by the Roswell citizen investigators should be excluded from the investigation.

> *"Many of these claims appear to be, undocumented, taken out of context, self-serving, or otherwise dubious. Additionally, many of the above authors are not even in agreement over various claims. Most notable of the confusing and now ever-changing claims is the controversy over the date(s) of the alleged incident, the exact location(s) of the purported debris, and the extent of the wreckage."*
>
> The Roswell Report 1995

While Cavitt had been interviewed by other Roswell UFO investigators, his official statements to Air Force investigators did not lead us any further to the truth in the matter. In fact, he initially denied being at RAAF at the time! It was only later, in the Air Force version of *The Roswell Report*, that he admitted to going out to the Foster Ranch. And I say this because when being interviewed by the author of *The Roswell Report*, Air Force Colonel Richard Weaver, Cavitt maintained that the material in the photos order by General Ramey in Fort Worth was the material he stated he recovered on the Foster Ranch. This we know to not be truthful or at the very least inaccurate, based on General DuBose reported statement that the weather balloon was a cover story, and it would only make sense to replace the material with random weather balloon parts. This could have been a mistake of fact on the part of Cavitt having to rely solely on his memory of things that happened decades before or is/was his continuing deception of the facts of the case.

Based on training and experience, I tend to believe General DuBose above all others. He was second in charge when the original material was received from Roswell to the Fort Worth Army Airfield. He would have been very aware of this deception and the replacing of the original material with the balloon material. On the other hand, Cavitt did not go to Fort Worth. While Marcel might have told him what had transpired when he arrived and met with Ramey, it may not have registered as especially important in Cavitt's mind.

Or as I said, he is continuing his deception.

When interviewing a potential reluctant witness, the investigator has to be acutely aware of how the interaction plays out. In such cases, a witness can tell you I don't want to talk to you anymore, get off my lawn, and there's nothing you can do about it. So it's in the interviewer's best interest to develop a professional, respectful, and friendly rapport with the interviewee. However, a professional interviewer needs to steer clear of disparaging other people whom he has interviewed, other investigators, and to ensure that they do not detract from the information provided by the witness. When an interviewer attaches an opinion, emotion, or criticism toward other witnesses or circumstances in the case, it can directly influence the person they are currently interviewing.

Before I appear to go on the attack of the Air Force's explanation in the document titled *The Roswell Report – Fact versus Fiction in the New Mexico Desert*, I will say that the authors of the report, Col. Weaver and Lt. McAndrew, compiled an impressive amount of documentation and constructed a compelling argument for the MOGUL explanation. However, in doing so, they lessened their credibility within the UFO and conspiracy communities by never once taking the UFO or alien theory seriously or further pursuing those lines of inquiry of people who were willing to present sworn eyewitness testimony to the case. Unfortunately, many of their report findings are diluted by their borderline sarcasm and overt cynicism of the extraterrestrial topic. I get it. In many of the cases I investigated, I had strong personal opinions; I just refrained from letting them guide my investigation or damage the facts.

The Air Force's disregard of the vast amount of witness information of more than one crash site not only leaves holes in the search, but it also insults the very citizens who affirm it is true. I understand that in Weaver and McAndrew's process, they chose to avoid addressing line for line the extraterrestrial assertions made by many book authors and independent investigators. I agree, it would have been inefficient and extremely time consuming. However, merely passing up the hints of UFO involvement and the utter ignoring of certain credible witnesses and evidence appeared disingenuous.

Using the Air Force's own logic, it would only make sense that there would be more than one crash site or debris field. If an entire MOGUL balloon train were approximately 657 feet long, taller than the Washington Monument and half the height of the Eiffel Tower, it is glaringly obvious that the entire contraption would not fit in a twenty-foot-long area as reported by Cavitt. Therefore, Cavitt's description is in opposition of the Air Force's own assertion that it was MOGUL, and he is therefore maintaining it was the weather balloon explanation, already exposed as a hoax. In this line of thinking, the Air Force would have to be wrong by maintaining there was only one recovery site if the Foster site were only twenty feet long. Oddly enough, the Air Force investigators just accept Cavitt's twenty-foot-long debris field description and move on, never thoroughly addressing this glaring disparity. If it was MOGUL, as the Air Force theorizes, we are missing an additional 637 feet of harnessing material, balloon parts, radar reflectors, and presumably electronics.

During official interviews, the Air Force men would often front-load their questions with a lot of information that had been gathered from other sources and other witnesses. Doing this, an investigator can be accused of steering the witness's answers or at least providing the necessary ideas they can build their answer upon. In reading the interview with Cavitt, I got the feeling that Cavitt's interview was more about a formality of interviewing someone to obtain a preconceived outcome rather than glean new information and bring light to the facts of the incident. In the Air Force's leading questions, it is quite obvious that they influenced Cavitt's answers, and in some cases guided Cavitt toward the answer they were seeking. However, this is not surprising—many investigators approach their work in more of a case management style than an investigative style. More of fill in the blanks and check the boxes than seek new information. This is a very militaristic and bureaucratic investigative approach. Already have the conclusion to your investigation before you begin, then build your investigation to support your conclusion.

Here is an example from the Air Force interview with Cavitt, as outlined in *The Roswell Report*:

Weaver: "*I guess they (referring to Roswell Incident citizen investigators) don't. That's the problem we have with this whole line of inquiry and attempt to look [at] this. It is very hard to prove the negative. It is hard to prove that something didn't happen, because you don't document stuff that doesn't happen.*"

Cavitt: "*No, it is pretty hard to, difficult, but a good imagination can. These boys (the Roswell Incident citizen investigators) have it (referring to good imagination).*"

Mrs. Cavitt: "*The picture that was in the Roswell paper, as I said, we had just gotten there so we probably had to start subscribing to it. But nobody passed it around.*"

Weaver: "Well let me tell you what's in the official records that we found so far. So you will have a feel."

Cavitt: "Please do."

Weaver: "We did this, as investigators would, logically. We figured, 'where would this stuff be'? So we went to all the different records. Working for me I have a group of reservists who are declassification experts. They are excellent researchers. They spend their whole time dealing with records, so these people know where all this stuff is buried. So, we have been to all the major record centers. The Archives and nuclear records (ranging from unclassified to TS nuclear stuff because the 509th was the only nuclear unit in the world at that time. So, some of there [sic] records were TS and still are.) That is because they have never been declassified. Anyway, we found that there was no airplane crash that could account for this. Just to show you how unsafe it was to fly at that time, there were six airplane crashes in less than a month in New Mexico alone in 1947, and that doesn't include the rest of the United States. We were lucky to have six."

Cavitt: "Remind me to double back on that. Go ahead with your story and I'll tell you another little story."

Weaver: "We found no indication of a V-2 launch that is not accounted for. There was one scheduled on the 3rd of July and that was scrubbed. There was no indication that there was some sort of nuclear accident at that time where we either dropped a weapon or did something stupid, which we had to consider during that period of time, but there is no indication of any of that happening. Weather balloon[s] themselves are; (although they have a 'return to' type of thing on them) supposed to crash. I mean, they go up and then sooner or later they're going to come down. Right? Now what we did find, however (and I not implying what you saw up there), but it's a possibility. There was a project run by New York University, out of Holloman at that time. It was a balloon experiment that

90

lasted for years. But at the time a portion of it was Top Secret.
It has since then declassified. It was called Project Mogul."

Cavitt: *"Never heard of it."*

Throughout the interview and line of questioning with Cavitt and his wife, the Air Force investigators maintain a loose and cavalier approach—more along the lines of him and Cavitt working out a plausible explanation and steering clear of any possible extraterrestrial involvement. In other words, the Air Force tactic indicates that they are building a case for the MOGUL explanation as opposed to an intent to collect and follow all investigative leads. A *'let's get this wrapped up and done'* attitude. This was never more poignant than when they presented a preface of the government's findings to Cavitt. If there was ever an argument for an investigator coaching a witness, this is it:

Weaver: *"Well let me tell you what's in the official records that we found so far. So you will have a feel."*

Sorry, but this has to be said: *Holy shit!*
Really?
If an investigator in a criminal case ever did this, it would be possible that the presiding judge would strike this witness's entire testimony from the record! If this is the interview on the record, based on such missteps, there is no telling what their communication was off the record. God bless all the Air Force personnel involved in this investigation. I know they had a tough job to do, but these types of oversights or intended strategies are apparent throughout the document and manifest an unprece-dented bias in a government-conducted investigation.

As I've said before, the Air Force's interview with Cavitt seemed to be more of a formality, a kind of check-the-box step with Cavitt, just to try to clear up any misunderstandings in reference to the Air Force's impending explanation of the event. Let's make sure you are clear on what we are going to report, that way you can be in lockstep with our findings...

Though limited in scope, it has been my experience working with members of the Air Force Office of Special Investigations (OSI) and the US Navy's Naval Investigative Services (NIS), their special agents and investigators are taught a very bureaucratic and structured interview and investigative style. Military investigations are often geared much more toward a governmental documentation platform than ferreting out and determining criminal or civil culpability. I know I will get a lot of criticism for saying this; however, I've watched these men at work and have been involved and knew the correct outcome in cases that these investigators were proven absolutely incorrect in their summations. I spent many years of my life serving in the military, and I am a United States military supporter. However, like many other things, we can have holes in our game.

It is rare that military personnel spend much more than three years in any assignment; therefore they are seriously lacking interviewing skills when compared to a law enforcement officer who has been investigating murders for twenty or thirty years. In the military, personnel are forced to advance; if they do not, they are ultimately mustered out. While this provides the personnel with a broader knowledge of their field, it does not afford them the opportunity to master some aspects, especially when it comes to specialized skill sets.

It is quite obvious that the Air Force's pursuit was in the direction of debunking and not considering any testimony that would suggest an extraterrestrial possibility. This is most notably indicated by his insinuations of the Roswell citizen investigators as being unprofessional or merely attempting to make a financial living off of the perpetuation of a hoax. That is as hard to prove as a UFO crash itself.

There is no doubt throughout the years, when citizen investigators gathered much of their information, there have been witness credibility questions. However, additional Air Force interviews should have been conducted for nothing more than an ability to eliminate the UFO plausibility—by not doing so, they did not eliminate it, and it firmly remains. In the Air Force's own words, you don't document what doesn't happen. Their minimization of the witness accounts of material other than what was pictured in General Ramey's office (confirmed by General DuBose's accounts of the incident) was a stark over-sight...a misstep in their philosophy. Had they addressed some of the more plausible assertions by Roswell witnesses, they could have addressed their statements and officially discredited them or debunked their interpretation of what they experienced. As is, these possibilities linger and are an obstruction to the case's closure.

Possibly the most glaring error is the utter absence of General DuBose's video testimony from the report. His name only appears in the 1994 Professor Charles Moore interview conducted presumably by Air Force Col. Jeff Butler and Lt. Jim McAndrew. The mention of DuBose addressed nothing in detail and was not expanded upon. And as accusatory as DuBose's statements were, they still did not address these assertions with Cavitt.

This is an overly concerning omission.

It borderlines on insulting the intelligence of the reader.

Keep on moving... Nothing to see here...

Based on the information gained from Cavitt's interviews, we can assert the following facts according to his testimony:

1. Cavitt checked out a jeep from the motor pool (not a Carryall).
2. He drove to the Foster Ranch.
3. He, Marcel, and Rickett located a twenty-foot-long small area with some debris.

4. The men picked up a small amount of debris consisting of bamboo sticks, reflecting material, and a black box (only reference).
5. Cavitt identified the small black box as a possible weather instrument.
6. The men returned the material to the intel/counterintel office.
7. Upon review, they identified the debris as parts of a weather balloon.
8. Cavitt did not write a report because it was a nonevent (even though it was reported on the AP worldwide as a captured flying disk).

I will say again, Air Force investigators had a tough job. But the Air Force's approach of coaching the witness and guiding of the interview gave the government conspiracists and Roswell focused ufologists exactly what they expected—and what I expected, frankly. A very deserving doubt in the Air Force's ability to remain objective and open. However, to Col. Weaver's credit, in retirement he has written his own account of the investigation he headed, leading up to the culmination of *The Roswell Report*. You can find his book on Amazon called: *Backstory: Roswell: Exclusive Untold Disclosures about the 1994 Air Force Roswell Report Told by the Man Who Led the Inquiry*. In it, he discussed the attempts at influence and manipulation he faced from the UFO community during and after the investigation among other controversies. He also discusses some regrets, which makes me pleased to see he is open to introspection and not totally narrowminded.

As far as Cavitt is concerned, he maintains what he, Marcel, and Rickett recovered from the Foster Ranch was a weather balloon, not a MOGUL balloon train. To the end of his days, Cavitt upheld that the Roswell Incident was nothing more than a routine event for members of the RAAF, and in his own sworn written statement to Colonel Weaver contained in *The Roswell Report*:

> *"... this whole incident was as [sic] no big deal and certainly did not involve anything extraterrestrial."*
>   Col. Sheridan Cavitt (Ret.)

Roswell
(1 page)

TELETYPE

FBI DALLAS   7-8-47   6-17 PM

DIRECTOR AND SAC, CINCINNATI   URGENT

FLYING DISC, INFORMATION CONCERNING.   HEADQUARTERS

EIGHTH AIR FORCE, TELEPHONICALLY ADVISED THIS OFFICE THAT AN OBJECT
PURPORTING TO BE A FLYING DISC WAS RE COVERED NEAR ROSWELL, NEW
MEXICO, THIS DATE. THE DISC IS HEXAGONAL IN SHAPE AND WAS SUSPENDED
FROM A BALLOON BY CABLE, WHICH BALLON WAS APPROXIMATELY TWENTY
FEET IN DIAMETER. ████████ FURTHER ADVISED THAT THE OBJECT
FOUND RESEMBLES A HIGH ALTITUDE WEATHER BALLOON WITH A RADAR
REFLECTOR, BUT THAT TELEPHONIC CONVERSATION BETWEEN THEIR OFFICE
AND WRIGHT FIELD HAD NOT ████████ BORNE OUT THIS BELIEF. DISC AND
BALLOON BEING TRANSPORTED TO WRIGHT FIELD BY SPECIAL PLANE FOR EXAMINATI
INFORMATION PROVIDED THIS OFFICE BECAUSE OF NATIONAL INTEREST IN CASE
████ AND FACT THAT NATIONAL BROADCASTING COMPANY, ASSOCIATED PRESS, AND
OTHERS ATTEMPTING TO BREAK STORY OF LOCATION OF DISC TODAY. ████
████ ADVISED WOULD REQUEST WRIGHT FIELD TO ADVISE CINCINNATI
OFFICE RESULTS OF EXAMINATION. NO FURTHER INVESTIGATION BEING
CONDUCTED.

                  WYLY
END   RECORDED
C:XXX ACK IN ORDER   JUL 22 1947
UA 92 FBI CI MJW
DPI H8
8-38 PM O
6-22 PM OK FBI WASH D
OK FBI

FBI Teletype - Courtesy of FBI FOIA Library

95

If that was the case, why did he not tell this to Marcel and Rickett at the time?

Just a thought...

And I must say, I agree with Col. Weaver, for whatever reason, Cavitt maintained his integrity, and maybe his honesty. All he had to do was wink, shake hands, smile for the cameras, and go to the bank (Weaver 156).

He did not chase the fame or the pot of gold—which was very easily in his reach.

10

A MAN IN THE THICK OF IT – LEWIS "BILL" RICKETT

COUNTERINTELLIGENCE MASTER SERGEANT, 509TH, RAAF,
ROSWELL, NEW MEXICO

"Rickett, according to popular myth, went out on the day of the press release to the crash site with Sheridan Cavitt."

Master Sergeant Lewis "Bill" Rickett

THIS IS A QUOTE FROM TIM PRINTY'S WEBSITE, astronomyufo.com, in his article titled, *"The Joker and the Spaceship."* The article is an example of front-loading research with an emotional personal opinion—sensational journalism. While many scientific papers will begin with an "abstract," the aims and outcomes of the research, it is typically written devoid of an emotional twist. Using an emotional appeal is a type of psychological conditioning that puts the reader into a position that can make them feel silly or stupid from the beginning for ever believing whatever is being disputed. Don't get me wrong, with Tim's background in astronomy and an over average amount of observable experience, we would want his knowledgeable and his well-informed deduction based on the facts—just not based on personal cynicism.

I have read everything on Tim's current website and enjoy his pragmatic, logical, and skeptical points of view. He is one of the men we need delving into the UFO phenomenon. Men like Tim Printy hold all ufologists to a higher requirement and challenge researchers to stick to industry standard methods of evidence observation and collection. Simply using human observation and amateur speculation does not pave the way to a credible conclusion, especially in the domain of ufology. These aerial accidental discharges do happen. One recent example was in 2018 when a military C-130 expelled a chaff burst(s) that was picked up on meteorological radars in Illinois, Indiana, and Kentucky. A novice would have believed what his radar scope showed him was a miraculous weather phenomenon. But based on the interpretation of known weather behavior, radar imagery display performance, and on-the-ground observation, this radar contact was classified as a military countermeasure.

I have witnessed strange things in the sky and even stranger things on Navy air detection and tracking radar equipment. I have witnessed events resembling the "Phoenix Lights" over military training ranges in Alaska where A-10s were practicing ground attacks, in militarized zones in the Middle East, and near demilitarized zones in the Sinai Desert. While camping in west Texas, I have even been on the receiving end of joker military pilots finding campers using night vision, swooping in silent, going vertical, blasting full afterburner five hundred feet over the campsite, then disappearing into the night—the experience is a sudden horrific noise and a bright blue ball of light shifting at incomprehensible angles, then vanishing into the blackness. Most fighter jocks know this little trick. The technique was even demonstrated during the annual Roswell UFO Festival parade one year down Main Street—a fantastically fun experience to say the least.

Lacking military battlefield or training experience, it is understandable how a common citizen knowing only what Hollywood or the television tells them about the military may misinterpret such events as something non-terrestrial. Military aircraft countermeasures during stateside training exercises such as flares and chaff can easily be misidentified to the untrained eye and often are. These countermeasures are useful when a pilot needs to confuse heat or radar seeking missiles. The heat seekers will go toward the flares and radar seekers toward the chaff, in a simplistic manner of speaking. These are evidence of misinterpretations of real events and should be presented as the logical conclusion to the reported observation, not merely dismissed as a false report or some sort of rural lore.

The one thing I would like to address is the sentence Tim provides in the very first paragraph of his article:

> "Rickett, according to popular myth, went out on the day of the press release to the crash site with Sheridan Cavitt."

Now, when we look at this, Tim is using what he would deem as facts from the US Air Force's document *The Roswell Report – Fact versus Fiction in the New Mexico Desert*. I say this because he should. The US Air Force, a professional military organization, must provide vetted and accurate information in any report they present. In the case of Rickett going out to the site, this was confirmed by the Air Force report's star witness's official statement, by Captain Sheridan Cavitt.

The Air Force takes Cavitt's statement to be fact.

Cavitt testified that Rickett was with him the day they were summoned to the Foster Ranch. So, my question is Tim's intentional use of the word "myth." Myth is defined as a widely held but false belief or idea. You cannot rely on one thing that is fact, in Tim's case *The Roswell Report*, then dismiss other testimony within your own cited reliable fact as fiction. Yes, I am splitting hairs on this; however, it matters. When a law enforcement officer enters an investigation with preconceived notions of a person's guilt, they will fit the evidence to the guilty scenario instead of following the evidence to the truth.

I've personally experienced this.

We know Lewis "Bill" Rickett went to the site of the debris field because Cavitt said he did, and Rickett later said he did. Are the dates in dispute? Yes. Are the locations in dispute? Yes. But we are dealing with decades-old memories—we can expect slight deviations of two separate persons' recollections of the same event.

Now before you slam this book shut in dispute of my own observations, I ask you hang on a little while longer, because the timeline and story does get confusing. In later interviews, Rickett does refer to:

1. Other debris sites.
2. The debris is undoubtedly of alien origin.
3. They passed through multiple checkpoints.
4. Saw multiple pieces of debris.
5. Witnessed a huge gouge in the ground.

Most of Rickett's accounts are not substantiated by Marcel or Cavitt; however, extensive research has gone into his claim by many ufologists—none were affirmatively debunked yet remain very controversial in nature. Decades later dozens of citizens came forward to substantiate Rickett's assertions, yet none present the smoking gun needed to close the case of the Roswell event.

All remain hearsay.

Given the fact that the MOGUL balloon train was over 650 feet long, it would fit better into Marcel and Rickett's description of a large debris field than Cavitt's description of a very small area—the size of his living room. Marcel's description matched Rickett's better than the ridiculously small twenty-by-twenty-foot area portrayed by Cavitt. Once again, I infer that Cavitt was keeping within the original weather balloon story concocted by Ramey in Fort Worth or possibly by Ramey's superior, General McMullin at the Pentagon.

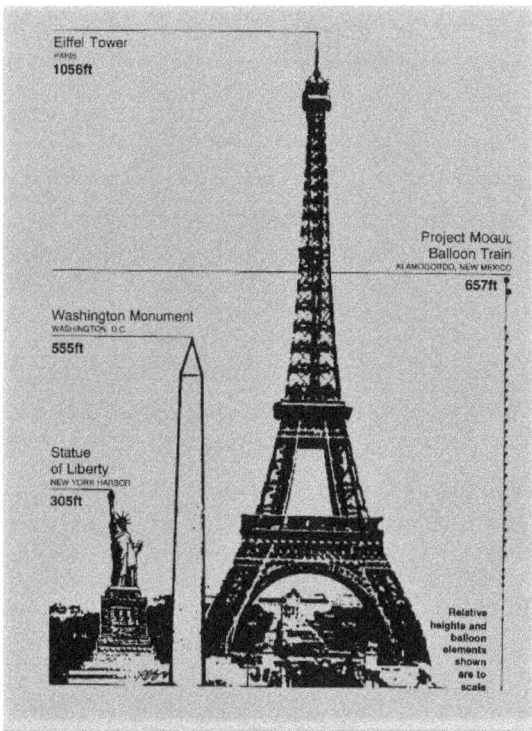

MOGUL ballon train comparison

On several occasions at different Roswell seminars and at the Roswell UFO Festival and museum conference, those researchers and incident experts discussed the memory metal collected on site. There is no doubt a strange and shiny material was gathered by the Marcel team; it was shown by Marcel to his wife and young son, then submitted to authorities at Roswell. However, there has always been controversy and inconsistencies in its description.

The Marcel faction maintains it was easily manipulated; however, it returned to its original shape on its own. The Rickett account was that it was indestructible and could not be manipulated even when tools such as hammers were applied. Could there have been two different types of materials described by witnesses to explain these discrepancies? These descriptions, like many others, seem to contradict evidence and testimony in the event. In many such cases, these types of inconsistencies would lead to an interpretation of untruthfulness on the part of the witnesses, whether it be times and dates, multiple locations, or differences in the description of the material involved. However, this is the Roswell Incident. It is unique in every way. It involves trained observers and untrained observers, professionals and novices, random citizenry, and children. A professional investigator would expect vast inconsistencies in the experiences of witnesses and contrasting differences in their interpretation and description of materials.

That would be normal.

But the circumstances reported do make perfect sense in the matter of various metallic compounds and multiple crash sites would be that of a MOGUL balloon train, or a high-speed extraterrestrial vehicle impact, or a high-speed terrestrial vehicle impact, or something else... Cavitt's description does not match the US Air Force explanation of MOGUL. Period. It would match the MOGUL train somehow breaking apart and impacting in various locations, thus creating what Rickett and many others would describe as multiple debris fields. The same with a high-speed vehicle impacting, shedding off material, going back airborne to one or two other impact sites before coming to rest at a final crash site. Like a stone skipping across the water.

These assumptions could also lead to an explanation of the different descriptions of the memory metal by Marcel, Brazel, Cavitt, and Rickett. If it were a high-speed initial impact, it could have stripped the outer layer or skin off the vehicle at the first site, supportive substructures at the second, framing at the third, etc. Scattering the differing types of alloys at each location could be the natural progression of the various crash sites.

Like many other post-*Unsolved Mysteries* witnesses, Rickett's story evolves to the point that he ultimately added witnessing a gouge in the earth and a long and thin crashed spaceship, according to a Kevin Randle and Don Schmitt interview. In previous interviews, much like Haut and Cavitt, Rickett was reluctant to participate and divulge any state-held secrets that may still be classified. But as time wore on and confirmation was provided that the incident was, in fact, declassified or, as some contend, never classified to begin with, Rickett added many details to his story.

Like many military veteran members, Rickett no doubt had a sense of humor about the serious situations he faced every day. Being a spy and a spy hunter of sorts during the Cold War, he would have been exposed to constant paranoia. Joking, laughter and "amicable" bullying is all an element of being part of a team that deals with face-to-face life-and-death decisions and situations. There are plenty of academic and administrative types who are quick to criticize professionals in the field for their unprofessional remarks or inappropriate behavior. But these are normal psychological coping mechanisms that unburden the contributor so they can do their job—not be obsessed by what they see or have to do.

I spent time as a child abuse investigator. Most normal people may experience minor knowledge or involvement in a child abuse situation once in their life. I assure you, detectives that work child abuse are exposed to horrific and unimaginable things on a daily basis. It is common for these detectives to receive several cases a day, witness several child forensic interviews a week, and routinely review vast photographic or video material to determine if a crime was committed. To not maintain some sort of immediate release would result in an unthinkable increase of PTSD cases, mandated psychotherapy, disciplinary transfers, and a corps of medicated cops.

Rickett, Cavitt and many others in the Counterintelligence Corps would be expected to have what some would consider other than normal behaviors as survival mechanisms—these men collected intelligence and lied for a living. High stress. High accountability. Sometimes face-to-face with other spies or traitors to the United States. The true challenge when reviewing these men's testimony is to determine where the truth ends and the deceptions begin. And in Rickett's case, toward the end, how much his health and additional stories he heard along the way affected his memory or his intent.

The one thing we should all remember is that regardless of Cavitt's description of Rickett's truthfulness and ability to weave a "tall tale," Rickett was at the top of his game in the late 1940s. With extensive counterintelligence experience, Rickett was assigned to assist the famous mathematician, astronomer, and meteor hunter professor Lincoln LaPaz. According to Rickett, Air Force documents, and LaPaz himself, Rickett accompanied LaPaz all over New Mexico during the 1948 "Green Fireball" scare. Their job was to determine what these balls were, whether they were a threat to America, and to locate one if possible.

You don't assign the class clown to assist Lincoln LaPaz...

[11]
THE UFO HUNTER DR. LINCOLN LAPAZ

PROFESSOR OF MATHEMATICS AND ASTRONOMY, UNIVERSITY OF NEW MEXICO

Dr. Lincoln LaPaz

AFTER INITIALLY READING THE AIR FORCE'S ROSWELL report back in 1995 or so, I became more interested in Professor Lincoln LaPaz. I had already read about LaPaz's involvement in several books and was intrigued by some investigators' suggestions that he was more directly involved in the Roswell Incident. I cannot find any explicit evidence that he was involved; however, this very rational man had experienced a strange UFO sighting on July 10, 1947, near Fort Sumner, New

Mexico. Oddly enough, this was only several days after the original RAAF's flying disk report to the *Roswell Daily Record*.

After visiting Meteor Crater, also known as Barringer Crater, in Arizona, I felt that LaPaz's observations could certainly provide some insight to the Roswell Incident whether he was directly involved or not. He is a man whose credentials match what he was assigned to investigate and report on. I mean this in a specific way. Often these days, people with a series of lettered credentials behind their name become TV pundits or talking heads, giving their learned opinion on circumstances in which they do not specialize, and somehow, we accept it because they are a so-called expert. Well, Dr. LaPaz was not just an accomplished academic. He was not just an educated authority. He was not just some experienced military contractor. LaPaz was an accomplished academic in mathematics—specifically trigonometry, which would be needed to establish an aerial object's trajectory. He was an educated authority in astronomy, eliminating any confusion of celestial bodies or anomalies that an untrained observer may misinterpret. He was an experienced military contractor assign to expertly identify and locate aerial phenomena for the United States government.

I point out these facts because there is confusion about investigators using their "expertise" in the area of unidentified aerial phenomena when they do have degrees in various philosophies, extensive training, and experience; however, they do not have these credentials in the categories or disciplines that relate to what they are observing. Someone who has a PhD in agriculture may not be the best choice if you are discussing varied wavelengths in the electromagnetic spectrum. While they will have a specific set of skills in observation, deduction, classification, they are just not specific enough to effectively investigate the incident in a way that would be accepted by the science or legal communities.

And that is what is truly at stake here, the credibility of the investigative process. The proper evidence procedures. The proper interview techniques. The avoidance of supposition in an absence of observable facts. That is what I am an expert in, investigative procedures. At some conferences they identify me as a ufologist. I am not. I am an in-depth researcher into the Roswell Incident. And saying that, there are many things I do not know about Roswell because I identify and focus on the people and circumstances that are directly related to the incident. All other information and data are merely trivia and nothing more.

It is vitally important that the investigator be able to determine vital facts from incidental facts. So often, Roswell researchers get wrapped around the axle on exact locations, exact times, etc. When, in fact, what is important is that we validate the actual event.

Without picking on anyone in particular, I will use myself as an example. I would be considered a law enforcement expert witness by any court due to the facts that I have a professional degree, have 6,000+ hours of continuing education (CE) and training in law enforcement process and procedures, have taught these disciplines as an academy instructor for over six years, and have thirty years of investigative and leadership policing experience. But those credentials only get me so far. Police tactics, firearms instruction and maintenance, investigative process, evidence collection and preservation practices, interview methods and interrogation approaches, use of force concepts, and the like. You would not want to use me for collision accident reconstruction, DWI testimony, or family violence investigations. Of these, I am not an expert.

Just Roswell and just those things directly associated. Even then, I can expect personal attacks from those who interpret this book as having an opposing view from their own. It is the nature of Roswell conspiracy. That is why it is so important that we gather as much as we can from the very people directly involved.

Back in 2011, Dr. Roger Launius conducted an informal lecture known as the "Ask and Expert" series for the Smithsonian National Air and Space Museum. He so happened to be the senior curator at the time and for whatever reason thought it would be a good idea to include a talk on Roswell. The video has over 104,000 views on YouTube at the time this was written. What he related to the viewers in the lecture was that he, Dr. Roger Launius, is not an expert on Roswell. He is obviously an expert, just not of this particular incident of topic. His presentation appears to be from hastily gathered pictures and notes found anywhere on the internet and heavily relied upon in his presentation. I am sure Dr. Launius is a good man, but delving off into the Roswell realm as an "expert" is inviting disparaging remarks and comments all over the internet—which he received. You can see this presentation on YouTube, just search "Ask an Expert: The Roswell Incident."

So let's get back to the real expert, Dr. Lincoln LaPaz. He had a lengthy history working the US government, more specifically as a contractor with the military during World War II. He spent time as a research mathematician at the New Mexico Proving Grounds, also known as the White Sands Missile Range. This included the Trinity Site, where the first nuclear bomb test was conducted. He has extensive involvement with both the US Army and Air Force.

There have been claims by post-1978 interviewees that Dr. LaPaz was brought in to investigate the Roswell Incident; however I have been unable to substantiate this. There are many other investigators who claim the validity of his involvement; however, I will leave this topic to their qualified defense. What I do know as fact is that Dr. LaPaz was brought in to investigate a series of sightings by New Mexico citizens and military personnel that greatly concerned the government.

During late 1948, a little over a year after the Roswell Incident, unidentified flying objects, later referred to as the Green Fireballs, were witnessed on trajectories over the Southwestern United States, more specifically, New Mexico. These sightings were often identified as UFOs due to their unusual green glow and were initially not classified as meteors. Up to this point in the United States, most experts in astronomy agreed that meteorites entering Earth's atmosphere shone bright white to the naked eye and were quite common. They rarely gained mass attention and were taken for granted as a frequent and natural occurrence. Bright green lights traveling across the night sky were something quite different.

It would be obvious that if UFOs were being sensationalized in the media, then more people would be looking skyward. And if there were more people looking skyward, there would be more phenomena seen, therefore reported. This would result in what would appear to be an increase in UFO activity over the observed area. However, since in 1948 this was a new type of observation, we did not have any previous data to compare it to; therefore, we really could not determine, at that time, if there was a true increase or not.

The interesting thing about these post–Roswell Incident Green Fireballs was that they intrigued Dr. LaPaz. So much so that LaPaz was not only tasked with identifying them but obtaining one as well. As the United States was moving into the Cold War with Russia, it was obvious too many that these observations could be from some sort of Soviet aerial vehicle or maybe even extraterrestrial. The hypothesis that the Green Fireballs were anything but naturally occurring events originated from the uniqueness of their color, their apparent slower speeds, and that they appeared to travel on a flat trajectory—all quite different from what the common citizen as well as the experienced astronomer usually observed.

In his investigation of the Green Fireballs, Dr. LaPaz relied heavily on mathematical trigonometry to identify the flight path as well as the possible landing site, should there be one. Previously, Dr. LaPaz had success in locating and collecting meteorites in this fashion; therefore he assumed the technique would work here with success.

I studied trigonometry while serving in the US Navy and in college as well. Precision navigation is primarily based on the principles of trigonometry, and being an operations specialist in the Navy, I used it daily with pencil and paper while working with maneuvering boards in the Tactical Operations Plot (TOP). Today's sailors primarily rely on computers—an extremely bad plan if your power fails. But Dr. LaPaz took the principles of trigonometry and inserted the variables of speed and the force of gravity to estimate terrestrial impact sites. From my readings, he was apparently intrigued with their flat trajectory. A flat trajectory would suggest that these fireballs had some sort of propulsion system that would maintain their speed and counteract the atmospheric friction and gravity that would normally pull them down. It was very unusual behavior when observed by the naked eye. It certainly differed from a common meteor.

While air detection and tracking specialists in the US Navy use advanced technologies compared to 1948, the math is the same. And so are the identification parameters: (1) course, (2) speed, (3) trajectory, (4) physical description, and (5) electromagnetic emanations. The course would be the actual flight path the object travelled, and the key question would be, did it change direction? The speed the object travelled and the key question, did its speed alter? The trajectory it followed and did it appear that other forces influence it? The physical description question was did it appear unique or anomalous? And finally, electromagnetic emanations—did the object emit any usual or unusual electromagnetic frequencies?

Those identification parameters are used on a daily basis in militaries throughout the world to identify aircraft as friend or foe. For instance, when a radar contact is traveling along a civilian airline corridor (like a designated highway in the sky), when it is traveling at a cruising speed of approximately 550 mph, adjusts its trajectory to maintain its course, looks like an airliner (assuming someone can get eyes on), and it is transmitting a common navigation radar frequency or radio signal, we can assume it is a passenger plane, not a hostile fighter or extraterrestrial spacecraft.

In his investigations, Dr. LaPaz did not have the advanced detection and tracking equipment used by today's militaries. But what he did have was an assigned counterintelligence officer from the US Air Force, a man known as none other than Master Sergeant Bill Rickett. The same Bill Rickett who accompanied Capt. Sheridan Cavitt to the debris field at the Foster Ranch.

Over the late 1940s and early 1950s, while working with other scientists and agents from the Office of Special Investigations of the United States Air Force, Dr. LaPaz interviewed hundreds of witnesses, both trained and untrained, civilian and military, ground observers and pilots, UFO believers and nonbelievers. Many of their descriptions were consistent, explaining the brilliant green glow and the flat trajectories of these objects. While LaPaz and many others never came down to positively identifying the Green Fireball phenomena, there was no shortage of speculation. In some of the cases reported out of Roswell were descriptions that correlated with the time and place of the possible event that led to the Roswell Incident. In some cases, witnesses described bright fiery objects that either fell to the ground beyond the horizon or continued its trajectory, either burning up or not totally entering the atmosphere and continuing on its space-bound journey.

Some researchers, including LaPaz at one point, believed these objects were not natural, possibly secret tests conducted by the United States government, possibly Soviet experimental or reconnaissance craft, or even extraterrestrial craft. Some even hypothesized the Green Fireballs were atmosphere-penetrating test vehicles launched from an orbiting spacecraft designed to assess the variables of entering the Earth's environment in preparation for their own landing—that is something we previously did on the moon and are currently doing on Mars.

Walker Air Force Base

Complicating things, there were WWII veteran witnesses who described the Green Fireballs as looking remarkably similar to the rocket blast exhaust of a German V-1 rocket. Thousands of these unusual, pulsejet, gasoline-powered rockets were launched against England during 1944. While they only hit their targets twenty-five percent of the time, they wreaked havoc on the British Isles. According to *Air Force Magazine*, this precursor to the modern-day cruise missile killed over 5,000 people and injured another 16,000 (Correll). With German scientists at Alamogordo, New Mexico, working on rocket projects, it would only make sense their experiments would match their previous technologies. However, there was one screaming inconsistency—the sound of the Green Fireballs was not the same as the V-1, also known for the loud and unique sound they produced, giving them the nickname of "buzz bombs."

Whatever the case, Bill Rickett and Lincoln LaPaz's contribution to identifying or not identifying observed UFOs over New Mexico helped narrow the search. In as much, LaPaz described Bill Ricket's contribution as a positive one. In a 1949 report to the 17th District OSI, Dr. LaPaz wrote:

> *"At Roswell, where very effective cooperation was provided by the OSI group at Walker Air Force Base under Lt. Paul Ryan, and the local CAP unit under Lt. H.K. Cobean, Special Agent Bill Rickett was added to the survey party and gave much aid in the later work."*
> The Roswell Report:
> Facts vs. Fiction in the New Mexico Desert

Dr. LaPaz's general and ambiguous word choice of "later work" was an interesting use of expression for him. For a scientist who is usually extremely specific with his word usage and observations, *"later work"* seems to be an uncharacteristically vague. In either case, he felt that Rickett's work was worthy of mentioning, as opposed to Cavitt's apparent need to discredit Rickett with his comment of *"... tend to exaggerate things."* It is interesting that Dr. LaPaz would choose to work with and compliment someone whose credibility would be in question by his former coworker.

According to Rickett's own testimony with Roswell citizen investigators corroborated by official government documents and a LaPaz's report, in the later 1940s Rickett and LaPaz trav-

113

elled all over New Mexico observing and attempting to locate the impact or landing sites of the observed Green Fireballs. Due to conflicting testimony by Rickett and others along with incomplete or absent documentation, it is unclear whether the Roswell Incident and the Green Fireball investigations were connected or whether they were mutually exclusive of one another.

Whatever the case, what is not in dispute is that Rickett and LaPaz drove around New Mexico in a vehicle and were the documented United States' Green Fireball hunters.

[12]

THE SETTING UP OF IRVING NEWTON

WEATHER OFFICER, FORT WORTH ARMY AIRFIELD, TEXAS

ON THE FATEFUL DAY OF JULY 9, 1947, WARRANT OFFICER Irving Newton received word that General George Ramey, commander of the Fort Worth Army Airfield, requested his presence in Ramey's office. In 1947, when a general asked for your presence, you reported immediately and without question —regardless of what task you may have underway. Newton did so and soon understood why his presence was needed. Assigned as the weather officer for the Fort Worth Army Airfield, it was assumed that Newton was an expert in atmospheric weather forecasting instruments. Therefore, he was summoned for one thing and one thing only—to identify the equipment that now lay on the floor of Ramey's office as a weather balloon.

We can confirm, by the statements of Jesse Marcel and later the videotaped interview of General Thomas DuBose, that the material portrayed in the now famous photo op in Ramey's office was in fact materials used for gathering weather forecast data—it was a weather balloon. There is no doubt of that.

The doubt and conspiracy that follows is: Was the material in Ramey's office the same material brought to Fort Worth by Jesse Marcel? According to Marcel, it was not. According to DuBose, the weather balloon was a cover story, and we can infer that the material brought in by Marcel was in fact replaced with the weather balloon material later identified by Newton.

This is the thing that is so confounding confusing. Not the fact that a trained intelligence officer would not be able to distinguish the difference between something manmade and something extraterrestrial—that's ridiculous. Not the fact that the Air Force would lie about a secret project, that would be expected. Not that the Air Force would replace standard balloon parts in place of classified material related to MOGUL and publish them in the media, that would be prudent. The confusing part is the fact that the 1994 Air Force Roswell report relies on the explanation that the material recovered was MOGUL yet maintains the material in Ramey's office is a weather balloon—while similar materials were used in each, MOGUL did have classified configurations and sensing devices not included in the photos. The fact that the Air Force Roswell report denies a large debris field based on counterintelligence officer Sheridan Cavitt's testimony, denies the explanation of multiple debris fields, yet says it was MOGUL—that a contraption over six hundred feet long with multiple instruments and multiple radar reflectors would fit in Cavitt's living room—even though the testimony of the scientists interviewed by the Air Force contradicts this explanation.

Throughout the years Newton has stuck to his story, and why wouldn't he, the items depicted in the Ramey office photos are material from an Air Force weather balloon. However, the fact that Marcel later stated that the material photographed was not the exact material he brought to Fort Worth is flatly ignored by the Air Force explanation. To me, this is apparent in the photograph taken by the staff photographer sent by the *Fort Worth Star-Telegram*—you can see a level of emotion in Marcel's eyes that is telling. Is his expression one of embarrassment that he misidentified something so simple? Was he uncomfortable because he was ordered to pose with a weather balloon that Ramey now says he misidentified as a flying (disc) saucer? Or did he then realize he was the fall guy for a military cover-up?

Study the photograph and you be the judge.

There are many versions of Newton's story told over the years; however the sworn statement gathered by the Air Force Roswell report investigation will have to stand as the official explanation of the events, sworn by the man who experienced them.

I believe Newton; what I see in the photos are definitely parts of a weather balloon.

When Air Force investigators contacted Newton in 1994 for their inquiry, he was a retired United States Air Force major. Newton stuck with his version of the story, which was truly his reality. In his written statement, he swore that:

> *"... I walked into the General's office where this supposed flying saucer was lying all over the floor. As soon as I saw it, I giggled and asked if that was the flying saucer... I told them that this was a balloon and a RAWIN target..."*

Yes, what Newton saw in Ramey's office that day was material from a weather balloon and a RAWIN target; that is not at all in dispute. The dispute in Newton's rendition is whether or not he knew the material was the actual material brought by Marcel or not. And how would he know? If he were brought in after the material was either replaced or swapped, he wouldn't know. He would simply provide his account of his interaction between the men involved and the material.

However, in his testimony, he provided damaging details that, either by design or fact, discredit Marcel's assertion that the material in the photo op was not the material brought to Fort Worth. In his affidavit included in *The Roswell Report*, Newton swore:

"While I was examining the debris, Major Marcel was picking up pieces of the target sticks and trying to convince me that some notations on the sticks were alien writings. There were figures on the sticks lavender or pink in color, appeared to be weather faded markings, with no rhyme or reason. He did not, convince me these were alien writings."

In this statement, Newton alone refutes Marcel's assertion that the material in the Ramey photos was staged at the direction of Ramey. If the material were staged, Marcel would not have the controversial material with the strange writing to show Newton. Now the debate centers around whether or not Marcel was incorrect about his recollection or being deliberately fictitious or whether Newton was mistaken about his recollection or continuing the cover-up at the Air Force's instruction. The truly odd thing is in the year 2020, Air Force lead investigator Richard Weaver still asserts due to sensational TV shows, the public continues to claim a cover-up (Weaver 196).

Hello? It was a cover-up.

There are many unanswered questions to the Newton/Marcel interaction. The key to this debate is whether or not Marcel's version or Newton's version is the truth:

1. Marcel affirming the material was not the material that he brought and was replaced at the behest of General Ramey, or
2. Newton's version that the material was what Marcel had brought from Roswell and his focus on the purple "alien" writings.

With both of the men dead, these questions are left to linger.

THE EXCLUSION OF JAMES BOND JOHNSON

FORT WORTH STAR-TELEGRAM PHOTOGRAPHER, FORT WORTH, TEXAS

Major Jesse Marcel, courtesy of UTA Libraries

119

IN 1947, JAMES BOND JOHNSON WAS A NEWSPAPER reporter for the *Fort Worth Star-Telegram*. On July 8 he was assigned the task to report to General Ramey at Fort Worth Army Airfield to photograph material related to the *Roswell Daily Record* story of "Army Captures Flying Saucer in Roswell Region." Johnson reported to the general, and after a short briefing, he helped stage the material and arrange the military personnel for the best photos possible.

General Roger Ramey, courtesy of UTA Libraries

There has been a lot of speculation and debate about the now famous *Fort Worth Star-Telegram* photos being housed at the University of Texas at Arlington. They appear to be the only existing documentation of the actual evidence reportedly found on the Foster Ranch. There has never been an official military report to surface by any of the personnel involved in the recovery, transport, or disposition of the material recovered. These five surviving photos seem to be the only evidentiary proof.

Major Jesse Marcel, courtesy of UTA Libraries

Of the photos, people have pondered the purpose of the staging of the material and placing the personnel inside the general's office. They have varying evaluations of Marcel's facial expression. They have hypothesized about Ramey's mysterious memo and its purpose in the photo. They have wondered about Ramey being the only person wearing his dress uniform. They have speculated about Ramey wearing his hat indoors—in his own office. But the one thing that is not strange is the military using the civilian media to get their story to the public. This would be the best and most efficient way for a strategy to cover up the previous disclosure of a flying saucer—give the people something more plausible, something easily believable. Then go silent and let time resolve to conspiracy.

General Ramey & General DuBose, courtesy of UTA Libraries

The Air Force tried and true answer, "The simplest solution is usually the best..." It's worked for them for years.

Since that day, James Bond Johnson's life has been one of a man with a mission. A reporter for a time, a career of military service, many accolades in academia, including a PhD in psychology, ordained as a Methodist minister, and the list goes on and on. However, in his later years, he became more and more interested in his part in the Roswell mystery. In his efforts to find out more and to get his story to the public, he reached out and agreed to do interviews with Roswell investigators and various media platforms. In one case, Johnson was corresponding with Joshua Shapiro of VJ Enterprises, who authored an article on their website called "Insights on Roswell." In the article, Shapiro displays an email chain between him and Johnson. In a portion of it, Johnson reiterates what I have been saying throughout my analysis of the Air Force's report.

> *"... I am impressed by the sincerity of the military folks I have discussed this situation with. I was not impressed with the attitude of the Air Force Intelligence officer who interviewed me in 1994 in connection with the GAO investigation in that he seemed to be just going through the motions and not too concerned with finding the true facts—his mind seemed already made up!"*
>
> Email Joshua Shapiro, VJ Enterprises

I was pleasantly pleased that I was not the only person picking up on this, and my experience was merely from reading the Air Force's own Roswell report. I imagine this would be much more prominent had I been directly involved with the investigators. With Johnson's statement, it is obvious the position the Air Force had taken was one of get this done and over with ASAP regardless of where witness testimony may lead you. In fact, if an investigator with the Air Force did interview Johnson about the balloon photos taken in Ramey's office, it should be included in *The Roswell Report.* This is transparency and gains the trust of all persons reading the findings in an investigation.

Having tunnel vision in the early process of an investigation can have damaging results. It will force the investigators to key in on certain people, places, things, and circumstances where they force these things to fit their own preconceived narrative.

Trust is paramount in a case like Roswell. The online *Roswell Report* that you can download is 994 pages long. And like many internal affairs investigations, it is filled with pages and pages of items and information not connected to the controversy in any way. They are merely included because they were in a document that contained a small amount of pertinent information. With a report nearly one thousand pages, it makes it appear the Air Force did an incredibly thorough job. However, they omit key portions of the transcripts of their key witnesses and exclude altogether any witness who may steer them away from their MOGUL explanation.

In 2013, Texas legislated the "Michael Morton Act." It requires that prosecutors disclose everything they do and discover in an investigation. It provides transparency and reveals any potential exculpatory evidence in the case. This exculpatory evidence might be statements, facts, or material that may absolve the defendant in a criminal case. In other words, they must reveal everything they know about the case, not just the information that will convict the defendant. Hiding or eliminating information does not lead to credibility. Concealing or excluding information is a red flag and damages the integrity of the investigation, sometimes to the point of invalidating it all together. For the last twenty-five years this has been the case. Cynics shrug their shoulders and say flying saucers are bullshit anyway, what's the difference if they believe the report or not? True believers say no matter what the government reports, short of total disclosure of the existence of UFOs, they are lying. And the skeptics say no matter what you believe in an investigation, method matters. If you are sloppy with your transcripts, inconsistent about your methods, and formulate the witness's official sworn statement for them, you lose credibility.

Everyone must have equal access to the facts.

The method approach from the Air Force on *The Roswell Report* was, interview and include only witnesses who can support the MOGUL explanation, bury the reader with supportive documentation of MOGUL, use the qualification of extremely competent but dead military personnel and scientists to support the MOGUL account, and exclude any witness information that would suggest a conspiracy such as the famous video statement from General DuBose or include an interview with the living J. Bond Johnson, who was a firsthand witness to the material brought to Fort Worth.

These are glaring oversights, and because I choose to believe the Air Force personnel researching this event to be competent, their method, or lack thereof, has to be by design.

In reference to method, any investigator needs to understand the industry standard. Things can vary, depending on the case, persons involved, and locations. However, there needs to be consistency in the approach. The true inconsistencies in *The Roswell Report* come in the manner in which the Air Force chose its witnesses and the way in which they conducted their interviews and documented the evidence. They had some events called interviews, some transcripts, crafted key witness statements, and exaggerated the thoroughness of their inquiry.

For instance, in the Air Force's interview with Sheridan Cavitt, they started off with the standard introduction of "who, what, when, and where." This provides context to the listener or reader of the origin of the information they are about to receive. "Why" is also a good thing to add in there in most cases. For instance, a professional criminal investigator would start an interview with something like this:

"I'm starting the recording. My name is Detective John Smith with the Metro Police. It is January 1, 2000, the time is 12:00 a.m. We are at police headquarters, 100 Justice Street, and I am speaking with Mark Jones about a burglary, case number 1001. Mark, please state your full name and date of birth for the record..."

The form isn't what matters, it is the content. And that is one of my biggest criticisms I have for the investigation. There was no consistency in the application of the interviews, the format in which they were conducted and semi-documented, and there was a lack of completeness in the transcripts, which lends serious credibility issues.

Each interview should have been (1) audio or video recorded, (2) professionally transcribed in its entirety, and (3) any affidavits formally sworn and signed with the clear understanding that the statement's sole purpose was to document only the relevant information the witness has about the incident. By not doing so, it made the report appear sloppy and incomplete—a jumble of semi-completed tasks. I remember reading the document in the late nineties and the confusion I felt about the laissez-faire approach the Air Force presented during these key evidence inquiries. The actual twenty-four-page official report completed by Col. Weaver was well worded, concise and to the point. In the report, it is glaringly obvious the Air Force never took its eyes off the ball—or balloon, that is...

Not a single consideration to the possibilities.

Excluding information gathered from J. Bond Johnson, one of the only remaining witnesses of the time, and eliminating information that could have potentially been gathered from him was a real mistake in the credibility and transparency of the department of the Air Force. However, the one good thing is, we do know he helped stage the photos, and he took the pictures—that is not in dispute.

Facts ignored by the Air Force, but not in dispute.

[14]

FEATURING THE MOGUL MEN

MOGUL MILITARY DIRECTOR USAF COLONEL ALBERT
TRAKOWSKI, AND NYU GRADUATE STUDENT PROFESSOR
CHARLES MOORE, ALAMOGORDO, NEW MEXICO

Charles Moore

IN WRITING THE 1995, *THE Roswell Report: Fact versus Fiction in the New Mexico Desert,* USAF Director of Security and Special Program Oversight Colonel Richard Weaver and Declassification and Review Officer 1st Lieutenant James McAndrew were assigned the daunting task of investigating the people, facts, and circumstances of the Roswell Incident. While I respect both men and the service to their country, the Air Force investigative approach was too narrow in scope to provide a conclusive report to explain the events, and if this were a criminal case, many of the witness testimonies provided would be impeached due to the manner in which the statements were collected.

According to the State Bar of Texas, there is a defined line between witness preparation for testifying in court and overt coaching. Ideally, the goal of an interviewer should be to gain insight in the scope of the witness's knowledge without impermissibly coloring the content of the witness's ultimate testimony (Terry et al. 2). In section three of ethical considerations, it goes on to say:

> "[The lawyer's] duty is to extract the facts from the witness, not pour them into him; to learn what they [sic] witness does know, not to tell him what he ought to know."
>
> In Matter of Eldredge (82 N.Y. 161)

The school of thought in which an investigation should have its foundation is something to be debated between investigators and academics. There are many differing theories of that approach. In some minds the method should be consistent and comprehensive as to maintain the investigative integrity of the process, and in others it should be fluid and driven by the circumstances. In some cases where individuals are trained in a specific mode of investigation, after many years, they come to the belief that their way is the only correct way to investigate. This is often the case with detectives who investigate in generalize crimes (theft, burglary, robbery). However, the more sophisticated the case, the more tools and methodical approaches the investigator must possess and understand when to employ them.

Sir Arthur Conan Doyle opened up this kind of critical thinking with his Sherlock Holmes novels. He explained sound investigative practices through his science-based investigations. In Holmes's time he believed a mystery could be solved using his skills of observation and human behaviors, and proper evaluations of evidence obtained from fingerprints, footprints, cyphers (codes or way of writing), handwriting, typewritten documents, and the behaviors of dogs (seriously). While technology has moved on to DNA, cell phones, electronic records and computer IP addresses, the behavior of dogs and people have remained essentially unchanged. It is here that the investigator needs to, in Holmes's words, use all your senses.

Colonel Albert Trakowski

An investigator's best tool is their brain, their ability to observe details and pay attention to the basics. Doing so will lead to an increased ability to comprehend the situation and get the most out of it. I have seen detectives pass right by a key witness, believing that they had nothing to add to the investigation—never pass up the chance to listen or underestimate a person. Holmes believed, *"It's a capital mistake to theorize before you have all the evidence."*

In Holmes's mind defining the mystery was the first step. In the case of Roswell, was it searching for a crashed spaceship? Was it proving that aliens were recovered and sent to Patterson Field? Or was it that a conspiracy was afoot? One of these will specifically lead you to the truth. Conducting the inquiry in one of two ways may lead you to the truth or lead you to what you want to hear. Using "inductive" reasoning means that you make observations of evidence or people and you determine your conclusion. The narrower your observations and the more hastily you make them, the simpler is your conclusion.

- Observation: Jim Ragsdale told lies about his Roswell experience.
- Observation: Glenn Dennis told lies about his Roswell experience.
- Theory: Roswell witnesses tell lies about their experience.
- Therefore, one would think the proper step to take would be to use "deductive" reasoning in which you

129

start with a theory and find facts to support that theory.

- <u>Theory</u>: Roswell witnesses are liars.
- <u>Observation/Premise</u>: General DuBose is a Roswell witness.
- <u>Conclusion</u>: Therefore, General DuBose is a liar. (False narrative.)

By excluding certain evidence or witnesses, we narrow our outcome and lessen the credibility of the investigation. There is a point you must stop your search; however, that is not before you exhaust your evaluation of credible physical evidence and pool of direct witnesses.

My original intent in writing this book was to concentrate on the key witnesses of the incident and facts that surround them—all of whom are now dead. They would be the citizens who witnessed the debris, law enforcement officials that became directly involved in the follow-up investigation and information dissemination, and military personnel directly involved in the collection, transportation, and analysis of the material. The problem with that approach is it is also too limited in scope as well. Like many Roswell true believer extremists, the Air Force approached the task from the opposite narrow "true unbeliever" spectrum. The Air Force did not come into the case as investigative skeptics, they entered into the task as abject cynics with the intent to do away with all this "craziness," as they suggested to Professor Moore. They concentrated on using official government documents and hand-selected witnesses to support their MOGUL theory instead of following the testimony and evidence trail to its conclusion. Although it is tempting, investigators should not theorize before they obtain all the evidence. Evidence will lead you to the truth. But in *Backstory: Roswell*, Weaver comes clean with his initial opinion about how the Air Force would need to approach the inquiry and report their hypothesis:

> *"Clearly, we had to do better than a snarky but true... response in order to answer the congressman's request, however goofy it was."*
>
> Backstory: Roswell
> Richard L. Weaver

Yes, evidence will lead you to the truth. I say this mainly based on four investigative facts of their process: (1) the Air Force used witness-leading techniques in most of their interviews, including with Sheridan Cavitt, and applied select portions of his guided testimony to much of the foundation of their own theory, (2) they maintained there was only one recovery site, using Cavitt's description of the size of his living room for a six-hundred-plus-foot-long MOGUL balloon train, (3) they accepted Cavitt's explanation of a weather balloon without further clarification, even after they had official records explaining otherwise, and (4) they completely and intentionally ignored General DuBose's videotaped testimony that the weather balloon was a cover story, thus contradicting their own star witness, Sheridan Cavitt. The very explanation of the weather balloon and that, in fact, this was the conspiracy.

And it was.

It is here I must deviate from my intended process and review persons I have confirmed were related to Project MOGUL; thus they may or may not have relevance to the investigation.

> *"Army Air Forces officials assembled an expert group of military and civilian scientists to carry out the project (MOGUL). The group included Dr. W. Maurice Ewing of Columbia University, a preeminent geophysicist and*

oceanographer; **Dr. Athelstan F. Spilhaus**, *the Director of Research at NYU who later advised five presidents on scientific and cultural matters; Dr. James Peoples, the Air Force's civilian project scientist and later editor of the Journal of Geophysical Research; Albert P. Crary, also a civilian Air Force scientist, known for significant contributions to Antarctic research; and* **Charles B. Moore**, *Project Engineer at NYU and an atmospheric physicist who pioneered the use of giant plastic research balloons still widely used today.* **Col. Marcellus Duffy**, *a respected Air Force pilot and scientific administrator, led the project.* **Capt. Albert C. Trakowski**, *a young Massachusetts Institute of Technology graduate, followed Duffy in the leadership role."*

The Roswell Report: Fact versus Fiction
in the New Mexico Desert

Unfortunately, by the time the Air Force began their investigation, only Moore, Trakowski, and Spilhaus from the MOGUL project were able to be interviewed. Both Moore and Trakowski referred to Dr. Spilhaus on many occasions in their interviews and the provided transcripts. However, when Spilhaus provided his official statement, it provided no additional or new information about the reported crash on the Foster Ranch. In fact, Dr. Spilhaus indicated he was unaware of the incident at the time.

Within Moore's review, I must point out that leading witnesses does appear to be a standard practice in Air Force investigations. When they brought in Air Force Col. Jeffery Butler, he continued this tactic—in some instances supercharging the technique. I am not clear whether or not this is a personal tactic of the investigators, a cultural behavior within the Air Force's Office of Special Investigations, or it is actually something Air Force special agents are trained to do to keep their investigation on track, but beginning an investigation with a summary of their previous findings directly influences a witness's testimony, and any civilian court of law would find the behavior suspect of witness tampering and coaching. They would most likely not allow any of the coached testimony into evidence.

But we are not looking at a criminal case. The investigation conducted by the Air Force had nothing at stake, no civil liabilities, no criminal charges, nothing. So there were no restrictions for the investigators to adhere to, just a narrative to directly and succinctly bring all parties involved to agree with the MOGUL solution.

In effect, in most of their interviews, they overtly lead the witnesses. Without completing a total review of the interviews conducted for *The Roswell Report*, I would like to examine several portions of some of the interviews conducted. First, let's take a look at a transcript with Charles Moore, the MOGUL Project Engineer & New York University Graduate Student, working at Alamogordo, New Mexico. In November 1946, Moore was involved in the Research Division of the College of Engineering of New York University. They obtained a contract, #W28-099-ac-241, with Watson Laboratories to devise, create and operate constant-level balloons for the Air Force Material Command.

Moore was located and later interviewed on June 8, 1994, by Col. Jeff Butler and Lt. McAndrew. It is worth mentioning that in Col. Weaver's 2020 book *Backstory: Roswell – Exclusive Untold Disclosures About the 1994 Air Force Roswell Report Told by the Man Who Led the Inquiry*, he stated in his absence, he hand-selected Col. Butler to do the interview with McAndrew. Butler's interviewing style mirrors Weaver's by front-loading the question, if there were any actual questions asked, with the investigator's selected facts and then passively allowing the witness, in this case Professor Moore, to continue the Air Force hypothesis.

Unfortunately, the way the interview was transcribed, it is

difficult to say for certain whether it is Butler or McAndrew doing the talking. I would have said, "asking the questions" but there is little of that compared to the amount of lecture or group discussion going on.

> Question: *You're familiar with the popular literature about the various crash sites. There's one crash site, two crash sites, three crash sites and all that craziness?*

From the very lead-in question and statement, once again, the Air Force is creating an atmosphere designed to put the witness (Professor Moore) into a position of intimidation by making him feel foolish should he disagree with the questioner's assertion of "... and all that craziness?" By including "all that craziness," Butler essentially discredits the Air Force's position by ignoring the fact that the material reported by Cavitt was obviously not over six hundred feet long; therefore common sense would infer there would have to be at least one more debris site.

There are hundreds of ways the Air Force could have asked the question without leading or manipulating the witness to feel silly. Providing questions for merely yes or no responses is either by design or through inexperience on the investigator's part. I believe it was by design. The following would be a more prudent and less manipulative way to glean information.

- Proper Question: What literature have you read about the Roswell Incident?
- Proper Question: What do you know about the location of the found material?
- Proper Question: Where was the location?
- Proper Question: Was there just one location?

There are certainly times that you want to narrow your

witness or suspect down to an affirmative yes or no answer; however as an investigator, when you are searching for clues, you often don't know the questions to ask in order to get a yes or no. Therefore, most of your questioning should be in a form in which the witness has to fill in the blanks. Using an open-ended questioning technique is key to stay away from leading and influencing the witness's answers. This will provide uninfluenced answers that the investigator can explore further.

> Question: *"What I'm thinking is we may have two incidents here, where they collected your debris from your radar targets, then there may have been another something else not related to a balloon."*

Does this sound like a question to you? It doesn't to me. It is definitely a passive statement designed to elicit a positive response in the questioner's favor. Trained OSI agents should be very aware of this, especially when dealing with an older man and his distant memories.

> Question: *"Of course the issue of the large area has been different in different reports. 200 yards, Cavitt in his description, described it in terms of his living room which was not that large."*

Interestingly enough, after this question—actually it was just a statement, not a question at all—Professor Moore disagreed and suggested that had it been a MOGUL balloon train, it could have filled a "reasonable" area. What a reasonable area would be to Moore is not exactly clear, but we can assume he meant larger than Cavitt's living room. After Moore disagreeing, instead of discussing the controversy further and clarifying the topic, the Air Force changes the topic to the construction of the MOGUL project, steering clear of any inconsistencies in the Air Force's investigative formula.

The next statement attacks the pro-UFO community directly. As a professional investigator, no matter how much you disagree or dislike someone else involved in the investigation, at all times, you maintain a neutral position, forever avoiding influencing your witness. The condescension in this next statement by Air Force investigators is specifically designed to discredit magazines, TV shows, and books referencing UFOs in order to get Moore to agree with the Air Force conclusion, not to provide clear and concise information. Do not misunderstand me here, there ARE plenty of magazines, TV shows, and books filled with pure conjecture, assumptions, and to be quite frank—science fiction. But you allow the witness to express these opinions, not yourself and an impartial investigator.

Question: *"Of course the people who put out things such as this journal, MUFON, Mutual UFO Network, the books that have been written by William Moore, and Randall Schmidt, and others, a lot of the popular television shows, they've just exacerbated the situation where a lot of things, quotations, some of your quotations [are] taken out of context. One of the individuals, Sheridan Cavitt, who at that time was a Counter-Intelligence Corps officer at [Roswell] Army Airfield who actually went out with Jesse Marcel to recover some material that has been alleged to be the results of a UFO which Colonel Cavitt specifically states looked like a weather balloon to him."*

One of the behaviors of a master manipulator is their ability to change the perspective of given reality—this has obviously been done on both parts of the "Roswell Argument" for and against the prospect of alien visitation. Readers of *The Roswell Report* can sit back and envision the investigators and others involved as just honest, professional men trying to get to the bottom of the story. This may be true, but I can assure you in a politically charged investigation there are many moving parts. In some cases, investigators who are told to reach a certain outcome must be calculating, strategic opportunists. I can say this because I know men like this. I've worked with men like this. I am not saying the Air Force personnel involved received higher orders to further confuse this entire issue, but I can say they went into the investigation already knowing the outcome they wanted to present, and it had nothing to do with spaceships or little green men—or gray men for that matter... They went in believing the simplest answer is usually the right answer—and in a thoroughly conducted investigation, I would normally agree.

At one point, Professor Moore states:

"I need to say here, you need to qualify everything I say with the memory of almost 50 years ago. I will say things that are to the best of my memory, but on the other hand, should other evidence indicate my memory is faulty, I readily accept that. So I'll state things to the best of my memory, but..."

At a certain time, a person's memories that are not regularly exercised or recalled decay to the point of becoming irretrievable. Corroborative questions are always beneficial in such cases. Time frames can be established by asking the person's address at the time of this incident. Where they were working, what car they drove, whether or not they were married. Questions about events that can narrow down a person to a time and place. You would think at the point that the witness, Professor Moore, indicates his fifty-year-old memories could be faulty, the investigators would modify their approach. You would think that the Air Force investigator would know such techniques. You would think that the investigators would utilize such techniques to clarify and narrow down the witness's story. You would think they would do this to at least appear to be thorough.

Nope.

They continue with front-loaded statements or questions in multiple succession. By no means am I suggesting Professor Moore's cognitive abilities or memory is affected by any disorder, I am merely stating when your witness informs you of possible lapses of memory, you move to a different approach that may aid in retrieving factual information. Let's review this next ninety-seven-word, five (5) point statement, consisting of no less than five (5) combined questions presented to the seventy-four-year-old Professor Moore.

Question: *As we've gone through the various research, what we believe to be Project Mogul was probably involved in this incident. The materials that were being used in Mogul included, of course, not only the polyethylene balloons, but included the neoprene balloons at some point, the various types of radar reflectors, the instrumentation that was being used. Is there any type of material from that project that you can think of that would be pliable, would be bendable, but could not be torn? Could any of the polyethylene or the foil-like radar reflectors, could that be the case?"*

In reading *The Roswell Report*, we do not know the feel of the environment in which Moore was interviewed. Were there distractions that affected his recall? Was there some type of external stress sidetracking him? Did the long front-loading of the questions diminish the effectiveness of his recall? Did combining multiple questions within a complex statement assist or deter from the effectiveness of the interview? Knowing how to read your witness's ability at recall is paramount in getting the best information possible.

There are many studies that support the more you ask a

question, the more likely the witness is to develop false memories of the topic (Cherry). The findings are supported through research of the American Psychiatric Association and others. In such cases it is beneficial to shorten questions, stimulate recall by exploring more about the answers that are given by the witness, skip over portions of memory that are vague but readdress them at a later time, and by no means should you ever suggest possible answers. If you do, it delegitimizes your interview in a significant way.

> Question: *"W.W. Brazel mentions eyelets which appear in the reflectors. There's also, on the polyethylene balloons, the shroud however you had it hooked on there. There's eyelets around the base. There was a ring at the neck of the balloon and then there were attach points to that ring, were there not?"*

and:

> Question: *"I know in Colonel Weaver's discussions with Sheridan Cavitt, they talked about the aspect of burning. He did not recall burning anything, but then his wife indicated that there had been one night they'd been out and had a barbecue and had a few beers and that Jesse Marcel just took a piece and stuck it in the barbecue and then pulled it back out. So if that's what they're using to say it wouldn't burn, that's what we consider typically testing a material for burning or not."*
>
> *The Roswell Report* – Moore Interview

Not to divert from my current course, but I must say, I have always enjoyed being a Monday morning quarterback in this case. I certainly would not have wanted Col. Weaver or Lt. McAndrew's assignment here. For six months of my Navy service, I was temporarily assigned duty (TAD) to the Master at

Arms (MA) section on USS *Nimitz*. My Operations Division chief found out I had been a cop before joining the Navy, so he felt it fitting that I serve as one on board *Nimitz* while we were transiting back from the Arabian Gulf. I was assigned and quickly completed my orientation and assumed the position as a night watch supervisor. Working with the then assigned Master at Arms division officer, I was quickly convinced that arrogance and irritability were the leading skill sets required for his position. This man was a horrible leader and an incompetent investigator. No matter what, once he got his mind made up, damn the facts! The NIS men on board were much more separate and lower key about their work.

These Navy men certainly had extensive training to be assigned to these positions; however, how much and how broad could their experience be on a ship full of young sailors? I know there was not a single felony investigated within the MA section during the six or so months I was assigned there. It was laughable to watch these men play hardball or good cop, bad cop with a nineteen-year-old sailor for stealing a Walkman or having a bottle of alcohol on board. Some of these men truly made their careers by destroying others.

Conducting a proper interview is about having the academic training of how an interview is directed and documented, getting the feel and experience through hundreds of interviews, and developing the instinct to read your witness/suspect's voice tone, eye contact, and body language to guide your next question. The Air Force seemed to approach *The Roswell Report* investigation more like a tabletop exercise where they used and guided their chosen witnesses to build the foundation for the MOGUL explanation. The actions were simply a formality to them.

Professor Charles Moore's entire interview is immensely powerful in support of the MOGUL argument. My problem with it is not Moore's age or recall, it is in the manner in which the Air Force personnel conducted the interview—an interview they knew would be going public for all to see. Imagine what else could happen in regular investigations with less or no public scrutiny.

The Air Force had a responsibility to collect and present the information in a logical, factual, and unbiased way. They had the responsibility to present to the public an impartial and untainted investigation of the circumstances. They had the responsibility to document their interviews properly—where was the interview conducted? In person or over the phone? At an office or at the witness's residence? They had the responsibility to at least audio record each interview and provide a complete transcript of that interview. They had the responsibility to conduct their inquiries and interviews in an ethical and non-manipulative way.

In my opinion, they did not.

During their interviews, once all the details were worked out, the clarification of information was provided by Col. Butler and Lt. McAndrew; they typed up a statement partly from information obtained from Charles Moore and partly from information supplied by the Air Force. Then the Air Force men administered his oath, and Moore signed the paper. Truth be told, their collaboration provided a very concise, detailed, and plausible account of a MOGUL balloon involvement—the simplest explanation...

Oddly enough, on June 29, 1994, Butler and McAndrew conducted an interview with Colonel Albert Trakowski, US Air Force retired. Professor Moore referred to Trakowski numerous times in his interview, and either McAndrew or Butler confirmed they had been trying to contact Trakowski but had failed to do so. Then Capt. Trakowski was the Air Force Project Officer for MOGUL and had taken over from then Capt. Marcellus Duffy and was instrumental to the Air Force's argument.

In reviewing Trakowski's interview, it is quite different in format and approach from Professor Moore's interview. The interview transcript is concise and obviously has redactions from the conversation the Air Force felt was not important to disclose. The use of ellipses in different sections of both Moore's and Trakowski's interviews had me questioning what was so unimportant or secret in the conversation to require a redaction of this information—if that was the case. In some instances, ellipses were used in a statement that is designed to infer a question, and the witness is expected to fill in the blank. (EXAMPLE: They would jump, and swim, and...) However, a transcript of an interview is a written account of that interview, and at no point should there be the elimination of words or the confusion of what is missing suggested by ellipses—even if it is the interviewer saying things like: "I'm about to turn on the recorder now." Everything should be included.

A sworn affidavit (statement) of an interview is far different. It is a crafted, written assertion of the important facts and circumstances garnered from the interview in which the affiant (sworn person) concisely describes the event as they perceived it to be. There is a difference—statements are edited, transcripts of interviews are usually not—everything said during the interview should be written down in a transcript if you are going to provide a transcript. If the interview was recorded with audio or video equipment, these mediums can be reviewed for accuracy and transparency. However, in the case of *The Roswell Report*, when the government is going to release a written account of the investigation, everything must be there in order to gain and maintain the public's trust.

At this point in *The Roswell Report*, it becomes more about the Air Force being transparent in their investigation of the event and less about whether or not it was a "flying saucer." Credibility is everything in an investigation, any perceived improprieties throw up red flags concerning the lack of transparency and the suggestion of designed deception.

In this case, the public could assume this would mean there is information covered that to this day is still classified or it is just chosen unimportant information eliminated by the government—once again. In either case, there seems to be either signs of deceit, a lack of openness, or a level of incompetency... you will have to decide.

While I said the Trakowski interview was different, it does start off with Butler front-loading a detailed summary of what they want Col. Trakowski to agree with. A simply horrible way to begin a conversation in which you want to collect unbiased and uninfluenced information.

> Question: *"We have [concluded] independently from several other researchers the fact that MOGUL is probably responsible for the so-called Roswell incident... The Air Force position on that is that it was a misidentified balloon. The balloon was not a weather balloon, but was then a classified project, Project MOGUL, which has since been declassified.*
>
> *What we have not found is any documented evidence that there was a planned cover story related to Project MOGUL. Jim has culled through literally millions of pages in various archives and repositories trying to find some sort of documented evidence where somebody at some level has stated that a cover story of weather research or weather-related activities would be used for Project MOGUL, the real purpose of which was nuclear detection..."*
>
> *The Roswell Report* – Trakowski Interview

I'm sorry, let's look a little closer at this particular part of his statement:

"Jim has culled through literally millions of pages in various archives and repositories..."

This statement by Col. Butler implies that Lt. "Jim" McAndrew has culled through at least two million pages of documentation since the GAO received the request in February 1994. This interview is in late June 1994—five (5) months into the investigation.

To put this into perspective, Jim would have to read over approximately 110 pages a day, 40,000 pages a year, for twenty-five years to equal just one million pages. Do the math for the at least two million pages Jim culled through as indicated by Butler's "millions"—plural. If Jim reads at ludicrous speed, he may be able to do two million before he is eighty; however, I have my doubts. If you like, you could break it down further to if McAndrew spent fifteen-seconds (a quick scan to see if there is anything of interest) on each page how long it would take him to "cull" through one million pages, but I'm not. At this point, it's safe to say Col. Butler is simply using verbal tactics to bolster his investigation's credibility through manipulative exaggeration.

Being a colonel in the United States Air Force provides a level of certainty that his information is credible. Therefore, providing an unfathomable number indicating the extreme dedication and certainty of their conclusions, the witness would feel any questions about the thoroughness of the Air Force investigation to be an insult. Therefore, people most often will accept such statements at face value, regardless of their plausibility. This type of approach is often used by persons who want to shut down anyone's opposition before they even begin any questions. And to be fair, Lt. McAndrew had a team of personnel doing much of the record searching, none of which is thoroughly documented in *The Roswell Report.*

However, the interview does level off some after this initial coaching and manipulation. The conversation with Trakowski was conducted in a much better manner than Professor Moore's. In most cases the questions are short and to the point, allowing Trakowski to answer and elaborate on his thoughts. Of the questions with some explanation, they were not of a coaching nature and more along the lines of clarifying specific topics. It makes me wonder if the same man was guiding the interview, since the approaches were so different.

However, there were deviations and subtle indicators that there is more to the story than what the Air Force is reporting. Now I know some of you will roll your eyes at my next observation. You will say that is common phrasing—that it is completely innocent. However, in the Air Force's interview with Col. Trakowski, they did make the statement that they were concerned about the credibility of the contents of the final draft of *The Roswell Report*.

> <u>Question</u>: *What we're trying to do is make sure we are open to the General Accounting Office and to the American public as a whole when we publish our reports. So to all the people we've discussed this with, we want to make absolutely certain that someone has not come to them and said, you're going to get in the cover story. We want this to be as open as possible and get this thing resolved once and for all. There are going to be those individuals—as you have stated, the true believers—who may not accept what we have to say, but we just want to try to get everything out in the open."*

When you forensically examine a sentence, you are looking for word structure, phrasing, context, tense, and content. Let's break down the above paragraph statement, even though it is misidentified in the transcript as a question.

> *"What we're <u>trying to do</u> is make sure we are open to the General Accounting Office..."*

Why are the men "trying" to do this? Why aren't they just doing it? This "... trying to do this..." could be revealing the subconscious knowledge that they are not being completely transparent in the investigation. Therefore, when they are not formally guarding their speech, such suppressed patterns emerge. Relevant or not, such wording is something to note and would definitely be exploited if the phrase were spoken by a "suspect" in a murder. These types of cues in speech may not be the red flag you are looking for to prove someone is lying, but they should be noted and examined further. Later, they will be helpful in forming future questions for the witness or suspect to elaborate on the topic.

> *"We want this to be as <u>open as possible</u> and get this thing resolved once and for all."*

Really? Open as possible? How about, we ARE going to conduct a completely transparent investigation? If the information is declassified, why wouldn't it be completely open? This wording indicates that there are facts and circumstances that will have to be evaluated and may or may not be released. This is an overtly worded subconscious statement indicating that the men intent to omit information.

And they did...

Let me give you a few examples of deceptive speech phrases that would be red flags during an interview. These are qualifying type statements usually made in response to a question:

- Question: Did you steal the money?
- Answer: You know, I was raised as a Christian... (Christians can't steal?)
- Question: Did you steal the money?
- Answer: Look, I'm going to be honest, I... (Were they not honest before?)

- Question: Did you steal the money?
- Answer: Did *I* steal the money? ... (a repeat of the initial question—BIG RED FLAG!!!)

Before you continue with your eye rolling at my pettiness, let me put some things in focus. When a professional investigator formulates a question, they do it in a way to obtain specific information. While there are less formal approaches to information gathering, such as a simple open dialogue or relaxed conversation about the subject, the investigator must still guide the discussion toward the truth and the facts. Knowing that the credibility of the investigation is at stake, the investigator cannot be apathetic about their approach. They must stay on their game and avoid pitfalls with careless casual declarations. Failure can give away any deceptive tactics they may be using to gain control over the interview.

"... but we just want to try to get everything out in the open."

You would think after going through "millions" of documents, as Yoda would say, *"Do or do not. There is no try..."* It was almost like the Air Force was shrugging its shoulders, knowing that their report would not suffice. That no matter what they concluded, other than it was a flying saucer with four aliens, they would have detractors criticizing their conclusion and making new arguments for the extraterrestrial position. A "damned if you do, damned if you don't" mindset. The problem with that is you will have people, like me, who will look at a professionally done and thorough investigation and say, "Well at least their work reflects proficient interview techniques, competent evidence reviews, and comprehensive documentation." Then we wouldn't have anything else of substance to critique.

Not here...

That is what is so surprising to me about some of the interview transcripts included in *The Roswell Report* documentation. Redacted information or unincluded information? Coaching or leading? Outright providing the intended outcome to the witnesses before or during the interview? In some interviews, it is almost like the investigators are there just to tell the witness what happened and say they *were* there. Like a check-the-box kind of approach. Almost like they were tired, knew exactly what had happened, and were trying to just get it finished. Expert forensic interviewers and cross-examiners know this. That is why for years law enforcement officials would keep a person in the interview room for hours without a break, trying to wear them down. Once they are tired, they will make mistakes in their story. They will use phrasing that can be interpreted or manipulated in a way they were not intending. The problem is, a tired interviewer or one who just wants to get the process over makes the same mistakes.

One of the more interesting things coming out of the Trakowski interview was that he and the former head of the MOGUL project, Col. Marcellus Duffy, had a conversation in July of 1947. Col. Duffy had been transferred to Wright Field after his time with MOGUL. He told Trakowski about a man from New Mexico showing him some debris and asking that he identify it. He stated he believed it was material similar to that used in the MOGUL project. Additionally, he confirms Professor Moore's description of the pinkish/purple tape recovered with the material.

If you are to believe Trakowski's statement, this will contradict much of the information gathered that Roswell was a nonevent and no material was ever sent to Wright Field. This discounts the Air Force's denial of any flights taking the material there and bolsters the argument that flight records may have been altered or destroyed. Or possibly, in a less controversial theory, the material was sent on another regularly scheduled flight later in the month by an unrelated assigned officer.

In any case, while the Air Force appears to be satisfied with their interview with Trakowski, I am left with the belief there was so much more to discuss with him, so many more follow-up questions related to the man who questioned Col. Duffy. Even the use of regressive techniques to try to obtain more details or a transition to a cognitive interview approach.

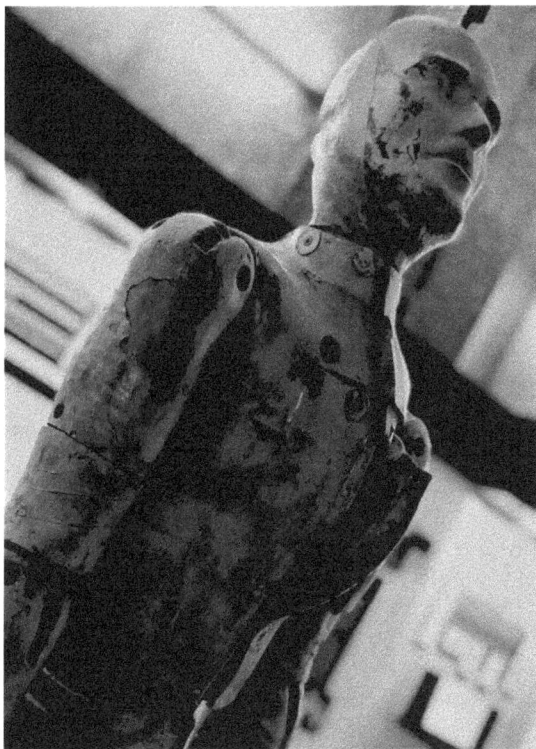

Test Dummy or Mistaken Alien

But like the others, the Air Force stuck to the rudimentary who, what, when, where, and how. Actually, they weren't even really doing that. Just a loose discussion about their MOGUL hypothesis. Then when the report was released to the public and was harshly criticized by many, the Air Force's later explanation came in the form of the "consolidated" memories theory. That all of these experiences by all of these witnesses happened at different times and different places. Then, over the years, the witnesses' brains simply merged the memories into a scenario that fit the more popular UFO/alien justification. Memory metal was foil, alien bodies were crash test dummies, an airman brought to the hospital were the charred bodies. Thus the Roswellian syndrome was born.

[15]

RABBIT TRAILS WITH THE HOAXER BROTHERS

THE SOPHISTRY AFTER 1978

DURING THE NIGHT, THE REMOTE DESERT IS A DARK PLACE. Even today with huge cities throughout the southwest, without a light source, one can see little. But imagine it is in late June 1947, there are no significant towns in the area between Roswell and Corona, no light pollution, no moon; just the stars and the ground.

It was a night just like this that **Deputy Sheriff Charles H. Forgus** reported he was with another sheriff's deputy and they were transporting a prisoner from Roswell back to Texas. Even today the roads in New Mexico are not the finest or best-maintained roads in the US. And in 1947 they were even worse, narrow, obstacle ridden and remote. Prior to modern highways and before the Interstate Highway System was completed, staying on the main roads would be key to navigating such a vast and sometimes featureless landscape. According to Deputy Forgus, he picked up radio information pertaining to a crash in the area of the desert he was driving through. It wasn't long before he and the other unidentified deputy soon drove up on a large group of military personnel, vehicles and equipment that were apparently controlling a scene. They came to a halt. From the car he could see a large craft, described as one hundred feet across, grounded down in the canyon. There were hundreds of military personnel moving about the scene, collecting evidence, loading the saucer on a truck, and maintaining the integrity of the scene. There was a group of military personnel extracting beings from the vehicle. They were approximately five feet tall, with brownish skin, and had large eyes. A short time later, military personnel instructed them to move on. Deputy Forgus returned to Big Springs and booked his prisoner into the local jail. Several days later a man from the government came to visit him. Forgus refused to speak with him about the incident and told him to leave.

The problem with Deputy Forgus's account is: It did not happen.

The incident he described to private investigator Deanna Bever in 1999 was filled with inconsistencies and apparent fabrications (Randle). Everything from the uniforms on the military personnel to the size of the craft, to the reported radio traffic about the crash is subject to discredit.

The crash site described by all other witnesses, both in the Roswell account and the Corona account, was on the opposite side of Roswell from Big Springs, Texas. There would have been no reason why Deputy Forgus would have been in that area thirty to one hundred miles northwest of Roswell. His business and route were far south of the location. Also, one of the biggest red flags is the fact that in all of the identified locations, none were located next to a major road and could be seen from that vantage point.

Whenever scientists or law enforcement personnel come forward to relate a fantastic story, it becomes even more intriguing. It is a fact that people know scientists and law enforcement officers both rely heavily on their credibility. To damage that credibility is to damage their career. Also, the simple fact that these individuals are trained to observe phenomenon or actions, collect evidence, and interview other observers is key to a credible investigation. This is why the interview of Charles H. Forgus is so intriguing. Being a law enforcement officer, he was required to swear an oath to honor and truthfulness. You would assume that he wouldn't intentionally fabricate a story just to attain a spot in history.

However, stranger things have happened.

Once again, there are two, maybe three ways that people lie. There are lies of omission, and there are lies of commission. If you want to, we can add in lies based on mistake of fact. You can do so also. In lies of omission the person simply denies they know anything about the event or intentionally leaves out key elements of the event. Lies of commission are fabrications of their involvement in the incident, or their knowledge of another's involvement. At the age of eighty-one, and not knowing deputy Forgus's health or mental status, we can assume he fabricated the story to establish his name in history.

Once again, this is a real challenge for investigators. They not only have to discover the evidence to an incident, but they must also wade through the chaff to get there. Just like in the previously mentioned yogurt shop murders in Austin, for many differing reasons, people will come forward to claim involvement for various personal reasons. Some cases are exacerbated by intentional hoaxers who simply want to become part of the story or are entertained by watching investigators head down the wrong path. Their motivations vary and not only complicate the investigation, but they also damage the credibility of future potential witnesses by their untruthfulness. Knowing these deceptions will occur, law enforcement and other investigative professionals must employ tactics to expose potential dishonesties.

There is no doubt that legitimate witnesses with controversial information about an event tend to hesitate to come forward. This hesitation comes from their desire to evade hostile cross-examination from investigators, avoid ridicule of the fantastic nature of their testimony, and the innate desire to avoid pain and punishment doled out by argumentative citizens and the media sensationalism.

To give Forgus the benefit of the doubt, in his advancing age, he may have confused a later plane crash with the reported UFO event. The Mutual UFO Network (MUFON) conducted an investigation of Deputy Forgus's claims and identified a US Air Force training flight that crashed in the area Forgus describes, six years after the Roswell Incident (Gross). However, that would not explain the craft measuring one hundred feet across or the aliens he saw. The true question about his testimony is, did he intentionally fabricate it, or is what he stated a mixture of jumbled memories arranged into a story that makes sense to him—something he really believes?

There are many Roswell investigators who have strong opinions about false memories. Numerous are extremely vocal, dismissing such accounts as being ridiculously fabricated excuses invented to discredit the testimony of professed witnesses to the Roswell UFO events. The problem with these oppositions is the people making them have absolutely no background in psychology. They simply base their belief on their own experiences and choose to discredit psychologists who have studied such cases and written peer-reviewed papers on the matter. Whether some choose to believe or not, memory does change over prolonged years.

I have experienced false memories and understand how they are constructed. In high school, one of my close friends used to pick me up for school on a regular basis in their red, 1974 Oldsmobile Cutlass sedan. I still have this very vivid memory in my mind—I can see it as I write these words. The problem is, the Cutlass was metallic blue, not red. Almost forty years after high school I mentioned the car to them, and they corrected me. I argued, and they pulled up their Facebook account and showed me a picture of the car and even one with me standing beside it. It was blue. To this day, I am bewildered by my continued memory of the red Cutlass.

False memories are the product of source confusion in which the content of the memory becomes disassociated from the source (Zaragoza). It is reasonable to believe I had a memory of a red car and that fragment of memory merged with my friend's car. Oftentimes the person experiencing the false memory will completely forget the source of the information and, in an attempt to make sense of the information, will construct a plausible solution by combining two related but incomplete items or events into one memory that the person can self-agree on. While Deputy Forgus may have once served his community enforcing the law, he will unfortunately forever be attributed to untruthfulness.

However, creating false memories based on what a person believes to be true events is different from intentionally fabricating all facets to a story—enter **Jim Ragsdale**.

I guess the one thing you have to give to Jim, if you are going to tell a completely fabricated story, you may as well make it fun and interesting. Jim certainly did this. He included danger, sexual tension, mystery, and plenty of intrigue. He led many an unsuspecting investigator down a pointless wormhole. As the story goes, while naked, Jim and his lover, Trudy Truelove, witnessed an object fly overhead and impact into the ground about a mile from them. They drove to investigate and saw a ship stuck in the side of a cliff. They decided to return in the morning when the light was better, making no attempts to rescue any survivors or notify the authorities. Once morning came, they checked the area, saw the ship, saw alien bodies, and collected some of the ship's debris before the Army arrived. Jim and Trudy hid from the Army personnel and watched as they cleaned the area. In later stories Jim went on to elaborate that he actually looked inside the craft and even tried to remove a helmet from one of the alien bodies.

Unfortunately, Jim reported that Trudy died in a vehicle accident, and the collected material she obtained from the reported spaceship crash site was not in her wrecked vehicle when he checked it. Also, his vehicle was stolen, which contained the debris he recovered from the crash site, thus eliminating any physical evidence to corroborate his story.

Plausible and convenient.

Unfortunately, no "Trudy Truelove" related to the Roswell Incident was ever located, dead or alive.

This is the danger of a witness not being totally truthful from the beginning of their testimony all the way through to the end. It is imperative that investigators discuss truthfulness with all involved persons who may be called on to make a statement. The investigator should explain that for a number of reasons, individuals sometimes intentionally leave out information they think is irrelevant or exclude information they wish to not be known. In doing so, if the investigator or other persons discover the omitted information, they may infer the person's testimony to not be factual. It opens the story they tell to a reasonable doubt.

That is why it is so discouraging when I watch videos or read accounts put forth by **Glenn Dennis**. Initially, Glenn's story made so much sense. It was so plausible and, given the circumstances, very believable. Especially when it is supported by so many other Roswell citizens. Many of whom testified that he had told them about his experience in or shortly after 1947.

If you didn't already know, Glenn Dennis was a mortician at the Ballard Funeral Home in Roswell in 1947. His information was of great value in Don Berliner and Stanton Friedman's *Crash at Corona: The Definitive Study of the Roswell Incident* and to Kevin Randle and Donald Schmitt in *UFO Crash at Roswell*. Glenn told his story many times, which grew and changed throughout his timeline. Ultimately, he relayed at least eleven events he personally experienced related directly to the Roswell Incident.

Glenn began his story at the Ballard Funeral Home where he (1) received a phone call from the mortuary officer at the RAAF asking (2) if the funeral home had child-sized and hermetically sealed caskets, and (3) they discussed how to preserve bodies that had been exposed to the elements for several days without contaminating them. He further reported later that day he (4) drove out to the base hospital and (5) saw strange wreckage in the back of a parked ambulance. While at the hospital, (6) a nurse he eventually later named as Naomi Self told him (7) she was a witness to alien autopsies at the hospital, and (8) she shortly thereafter received a permanent change of station to somewhere in England. He later (9) claimed he wrote to her, and the letter was returned to him, later finding out (10) she was killed in a plane crash, or (11) left the military and joined a convent.

Unfortunately, there is not a single shred of physical evidence to support his story, other than those anecdotes shared by Roswell citizens after the *Unsolved Mysteries* episode. I'm sure if you tried, you could find more than eleven easily identifiable deceptive statements made by Glenn, but eleven is enough for me. Now the problem with my assertion is that I cannot prove Glenn Dennis did or did not received a call from the RAAF about the caskets, make a trip to the hospital, or see the ambulance with strange debris. None of which prove or indicate anything about a flying saucer from outer space. What just about every Roswell Incident investigator has been able to prove is that the nurse Glenn Dennis referred to—the one he received the information about spacecraft and aliens from—did not exist. And as far as conspiracies, agents of the government would have to not only erase all military records of this person from the Personnel Records Center in St. Louis, but they would also have to track down and destroy every yearbook possessed by every Roswell service member who may have one...

I am getting an eye twitch just thinking about this...

I actually like Mr. Dennis. Inadvertently, his deceptions spurred a much broader and in-depth investigation about the many facets of this mystery. Without his amazing assertion that alien bodies made it all the way to the base hospital for an autopsy, we may have overlooked much of what was exposed during the research of his story. If you wish to go further down the conspiracy theory rabbit hole with Glenn Dennis and his supporters, feel free. I will respectfully exclude myself from further involvement. There is more than enough to read about him online.

There are many other persons classified as witnesses to Roswell. Mostly they simply share anecdotal accounts of (1) large convoys of military vehicles, (2) large groups of military personnel in or around areas the witnesses felt were suspicious, and (3) trucks loaded down with what some believe were air or spacecraft covered by tarpaulins. All activities that are good circumstantial situations that one could surmise the government was covering up the existence of a flying saucer.

Or it could have been something else.

But then there are the recounted firsthand reports of related events from people who appear to have no agenda in the manner of their alleged story. Many of these stories are believed credible by many researchers, due to the integrity of the witness and the conditions in which their accounts are related. A good example is the story related in *The Roswell Incident* by Charles Berlitz and William Moore. The story outlines information told by Vern Maltais that his friend Barney Barnett came upon a second crash site. Vern stated Barney described a disk-shaped, metallic-structured craft that was damaged due to having impacted with the ground when it apparently crashed. According to Vern, Barney described the vehicle was approximately thirty feet in diameter, torn open, and that Barney witnessed occupants of the craft among the debris, some in and some lying near the craft. He believed all four to be dead and described them as wearing a one-piece silver uniform, having small eyes that were strangely set apart, and having unusually large heads.

According to Vern, Berlitz and Moore, they felt that the story told to Vern was credible due to Barney's honorable standing with his community. Due to Barney's death in 1969, they were unable to interview him for a firsthand account. But Berlitz and Moore felt Vern was credible enough to use his testimony as a concrete building block in their book and investigation. According to the television show *Unsolved Mysteries*, Vern went on the record saying:

> *"Barney was just a real straight forward, just what you would call a real straight guy. He wouldn't... tell you a story out of color or nothing. That's why I was really surprised when he related this information to me about a crashed saucer."*
>
> *Unsolved Mysteries*

The problem with Vern's account is it was not corroborated with any additional witnesses or evidence at the time that Vern or Barney were still alive. And the story is impossible to corroborate now. Vern had stated when Barney was on scene, a group of university archeologists (possibly from the University of Pennsylvania) came upon the scene as well. But all of them were ordered to leave and not speak of the incident by arriving military personnel. Exhaustive efforts have been put into finding the archeologists by Tom Carey and many different Roswell investigators and TV documentarians. None have been successful. That's what makes stories such as the one told by Vern so frustrating. Much like a suspect having no alibi for the crime he is accused of, having no additional supportive witnesses or evidence does not mean what Vern said did not happen—it simply lingers out in the realm of possibilities but may provide additional convincing leads at a later time.

Then there are more overt fabricators such as **Gerald Anderson**. Shortly after the 1990 broadcast of *Unsolved Mysteries*, Anderson came forward with a smoking gun story. He reported when he was six years old, while searching for geological samples, he was with his father and several other family members (all dead in 1990) on the Plains of St. Augustin when they came upon a crashed saucer and two dead and two living aliens. He supported the Barnett story (that he had just seen on TV) recounting Barnett and several archaeology students being there also. Initially the problem with Anderson's story was much like the others—no corroborating evidence. But twelve months passed, and he recalled his uncle had written about it in his diary. Finally, the support the UFO community needed to prove the existence of the Roswell crash. He presented the diary, and it seemed to be just what they needed. Until it was researched. The paper was proven to be from the 1940s, but the ink used was not mass produced until the 1970s, well after his uncle had died. Eventually Anderson came clean and admitted the diary was a fake, shattering many of the Roswell researchers' assertions.

Being located in Texas, on several occasions, I followed up with some leads Tom Carey asked me to investigate. Two were located in Kerrville, Texas, and unfortunately neither brought us any closer to the truth. One was an officer who served at Roswell during July 1947. When I arrived at his residence, it was for sale, and I discovered he had died two months prior with no living relatives. The Realtor refused to share where his personal belongings were sent or whether they had been destroyed. The other was a daughter of a RAAF noncommissioned officer. While I tried several times to catch her at home, I was unable to do so. I left business cards on her door and sent her several letters with self-addressed return envelopes; however, I never received a response.

The final lead I received from Tom Carey was that of the son of a corporal who was serving with the "Green Hornets" at the RAAF in 1947—we shall refer to him as "**The Son**." Tom sent me an email that stated:

> *"... there lives in San Antonio someone who is potentially the most important witness ever in the Roswell Case. He's the son of a former 509th BG airman who we know was at Roswell in 1947 and who, according to his son, 'took pictures of everything' and took 'physical evidence' for himself. The Son told me that he is in possession of these items about a year ago. He has sense [sic] stopped answering his phone and has not phoned me back as promised... This is either a big hoax or the big breakthrough we have all been hoping for..."*

Tom and freelance reporter Greg Schwartz were working on tracking down some information on him, and Tom asked me to join in. Greg Schwartz corresponded with The Son and actually met him for a beer. According to Greg, they talked for about ninety minutes, and he indicated he did not believe The Son was a hoaxer. However, once again, The Son evaded presenting any facts, debris, or photos to Greg Schwartz and once again began to avoid further interaction and correspondence with Greg and Tom, saying it wasn't the right time for him to bring it forward. He also alluded that he'd had some earlier disagreement with Don Schmitt and that was one of the reasons for his full disclosure delay. By the time I became involved, The Son totally avoided meeting or any further communication after explaining that he had given the material of the flying saucer to one of his friends living in Washington State. Upon additional questioning before his complete avoidance in the matter, The Son said he'd sent to the material to his friend via UPS...

UPS?... Seriously? The Son sent the most important discovery of all of humankind to his friend in Washington state via UPS.

Roger that.

Crystal clear on this one...

Hope he bought the insurance.

Tom Carey and I had a lengthy email discussion about The Son in 2012. Tom had sent a request to me that I had missed for several weeks. Once I responded, Tom emailed:

"Thanks, Gregg. Better Late than never. BTW, our friend [The Son] in San Antonio is still at it—contacting other Roswell investigators with the same story. He even contacted the UFO Museum in Roswell with it. Go figure. Best."

I responded:

"If you need me to corner him down here, I can do it. If you think it will do any good for you or you think the museum would want me to. If nothing else, I can call him a flake to his face. What's the most he would do, not give the item [material] to you?..."

Tom emailed:

"The museum blew him off, so there is nothing to hold you back from confronting him. The big question we all have is, 'Why is he doing this?' Do whatever you deem necessary to get to the bottom of this. To learn the genesis of his 'act' will be a boon to us all. We have learned that his father's family was fairly rich, but it doesn't appear to have 'trickled down' to [The Son]. Best."

I spoke with The Son on the phone. I tried to meet with him

in person; however, he kept cancelling our meeting. Once I accused him of stringing me and other investigators along, he went radio silent. I have not heard from him since, and I have not tried to follow up with him. Should Tom Carey, Don Schmitt, or Greg Schwartz wish to relay The Son's real name to the world, that is their choice; however, I do not want to be any catalyst to a further waste of time or any infamy this sad individual may seek.

Don't get me wrong about lying; we all need to lie. I spoke about this at the Michigan Paranormal Conference in Sault Ste. Marie in 2017—needless to say I received some unenlightened criticism. Many people could not understand my example of maintaining a reasonable balance between total truth and outright lies. Many sociologists and psychologists study and reference such behavior. American Social Psychologist Professor Leonard Saxe says that lying—for better or for worse— is an integral part of life. Political leaders lie to get elected... people lie to their lovers (about previous experience, etc.)... they lie about their qualifications to obtain jobs, etc. Most of these types of lies are considered in the American culture as "little white lies." These are lies no one considers enough to be ethically damaging or morally hurtful to require any further inquiry.

They are just accepted.

Every day.

Where lying gets important is when it becomes destructive. Where it wastes others' valuable time. Where it defrauds people of their effort or their money.

Steps in, former Roswell Chamber of Commerce Executive Vice President **Frank Kaufman**. Frank was a well-known citizen of Roswell and had been stationed at the Roswell Army Airfield in 1947. When Roswell investigators were instructed by Walter Haut to seek him out, they did. The story he detailed was the holy grail of the Roswell conspiracy. In essence, Kaufmann relayed that (1) on or about July 2–4, 1947, he was (2) working with a radar unit at the White Sands Proving Grounds, 132 miles from Roswell—even further from the Foster Ranch, (3) the radar unit seemed to brighten as if to indicate an explosion had occurred along with debris falling to the ground, (4) was order to the crash site, (5) witnessed a downed spacecraft, (6) witnessed the alien crew, (7) helped recover the spacecraft, (8) assisted in collecting the alien crew, (9) transported the same to various locations for further study, and (10) was aware that camouflage specialists were brought in to make the grounds appear as if nothing had occurred.

In 1994, many of the things I read that Kaufmann stated he had done or witnessed did not make sense to me. It made me concerned for the credibility of Kaufmann's stories. I am not going to go through all of his claims, but I would like to discuss a couple. First, Kaufmann's description of the "explosion" as indicated on the radar scope. As I said before, I was an operations specialist in the US Navy. One of our main jobs is operating radar equipment. The actual rate (job) of operations specialist used to be called a Navy radarman. So I am familiar with the 1990s model of radars and earlier, which would not light up like an explosion on the monitor screen. The word "RADAR" stands for Radio Detection and Ranging. In other words, it can tell you the direction and distance of an object. Using those two knowns, the operator or computer can, if equipped, calculate the possible altitude.

One must think of how the radar technology works. A radar antenna sends out a radio frequency, that frequency bounces off anything in front of it, returning to the antenna, the computer calculates the strength of the return (how much frequency is returned) and the distance base of the time it takes from send to receive again, then transfers it to a circular display monitor that shows a halfmoon piece of video, the size depending on the mass of the object the frequency is reflected off of. This display shows only the area of the object that has reflected the radar signal. It will not show the shape of the object. In an explosion in 1947, the object that exploded would immediately begin to get smaller because it is coming apart and becoming less dense. The fire and gas from an explosion would be porous to the radio frequency energy from the radar and not be reflected back—it needs a solid object to reflect back from. Therefore, in 1947, if something exploded in midair, the only thing you would see is it simply getting fainter and smaller, ultimately disappearing, not brighter and bigger, then fainter and smaller. The other thing is the distance of White Sands as it relates to debris falling on the Foster Ranch or other areas in proximity to Roswell—132 miles away. If we are observing from a height of six feet, the horizon would be about three miles away based on the flat plain. That would mean the UFO would need to be extremely high based on 129 miles away. Which is completely possible since radars in the late 1940s should be effective out to at least 150 miles and at least 20,000 feet. However, that does not negate the fact that it would still not indicate an explosion by displaying a bright signature on the monitor. Current doppler technologies can provide a large signature indication of an explosion, such as that picked up on an Orlando Doppler radar of a Falcon 9 rocket that exploded shortly after launch in January 2020.

But not in 1947...

Then there is the fact that Kaufmann was assigned in an administrative personnel role within the US Army Air Force, not as a radarman. Not in intelligence. Not in security, etc. For me, Kaufmann and his incredible story has too many holes in it to spend additional time to elaborate further. Too many intentional deceptions, such as the modifications to his military service records, to spend a great deal of time on his story. Much like Glenn Dennis's deceptions, we just cannot rely on Kaufmann's account of the event, or his role in it.

That too is another frustrating thing about investigations

and witness credibility. Just because someone tells lies to an investigator does not mean that everything they say is a lie. It is up to the investigator to validate the witness or suspect's statements using additional witness testimony, physical evidence, circumstances, or technology.

Then there is **Colonel Philip Corso**, retired Army officer and author of *The Day After Roswell*. I actually really enjoyed his book. It delves off into UFO recovery, aliens, state secrets, and psychological intrigue. In his writings, more of a proposed memoir actually, Corso outlines his role in overseeing the reverse engineering of the artifacts recovered from the Roswell crash and how these extraterrestrial technologies became the catalysts for major scientific advancements in lasers, fiber-optics, and computer chips.

Corso asserts that he was the chief of the Army's Foreign Technology Division, of which his military DA Form 66 confirms; however, it appears to only be the case for ninety days. Yet, his book did not survive the scrutiny of UFO researchers and debunkers alike. Eventually, *The Day After Roswell* was discounted as a work of mostly fiction. *The Guardian*, a British daily newspaper, included it in their top ten literary hoaxes. Unfortunately Corso died of a heart attack shortly after the book was published; therefore we will never get the chance to hear his defense.

I think those are good enough examples of how and why the Roswell Incident became so additionally controversial and confusing. The odd thing is, had it not been for hoaxers and other completely unrelated persons trying to insert themselves into the story, the investigation would not have moved as far forward as it has. Elaborations and deceptions by Dennis, Forgus, Ragsdale, Kaufmann and many others exposed countless additional circumstances about the Roswell Incident that we would have never discovered. Most likely, many of the outrageous claims actually fueled the drive toward forcing an official investigation into the matter and opening relevant government records the Government Accounting Office (GAO) and other agencies had control over.

Just after a little research one can completely understand why the assigned Air Force investigators decided to limit their witness pool and avoid going down every rabbit trail laid before them. Part of conducting an investigation is case management—there is only so much time; you have to maximize your use of it. Using problem solving, management techniques, critical thinking, means of deduction, and a little intuition, investigators have to corral the information into something controllable. Reinterviewing persons of questionable character or who are known to be untruthful can be a complete waste of time, even if they may have some truthful information in their story. It is more likely investigators will spend their time on those witnesses with a high level of credibility.

But ultimately, no matter what your opinion of them, these hoaxers served a valuable purpose. They forced an examination of the credibility of the witness claims and the plausibility of the events that cumulated and became what we know as the Roswell Incident.

ROSWELL INCIDENT CITIZEN INVESTIGATORS, AUTHORS &
RESEARCHERS

Any normal investigation can pose its own challenges. Normal routine cases will always have some sort of turn or twist that the investigator must unravel. A normal family disturbance case will have a known suspect(s) but unknown causes. A normal burglary will have known motives but an unknown suspect(s). The problem with the Roswell Incident is in the beginning, nothing was known. This was not a normal investigation. To begin with, the investigation started with an intelligence officer, Maj. Jesse Marcel, as the lead investigator with a counterintelligence officer, Cpt. Sheridan Cavitt, as his assistant. A highly unusual manner of inquiry, which would lead a reasonable and prudent person to believe there was more to the story than "Move along, there is nothing to see here..." Then came a very unusual press release, which almost automatically turned to a complete denial the following day. Then the essentially thirty-two-year silence until Marcel's confession that it wasn't a weather balloon, it was something not of this world.

The Roswell tale has taken many twists and turns through the years. Sometimes the story was structured by firsthand witnesses like Brazel, Marcel, and DuBose; other times it was fueled by Good Samaritans who believed they saw something related to the incident, heard a friend or family member speak of the incident, or are those just looking to include themselves in the incident in some way for some personal purpose. The motivations for each reported witness who made an official statement are vast. As well is the experience, training, and motivation of the Roswell citizen investigators. But whatever the investigators' true motivation was, their dedication to the investigation and perseverance in spite of their many detractors must be commended.

I have witnessed many a cynic speak about the Roswell Incident with contempt. Many ridicule the persons who have dedicated thousands of hours to researching, interviewing, and examining the facts. I have seen doubters roll their eyes even before the pro Roswell supporter opens their mouth to express the possibilities. When I see this, it is a constant reminder of media personalities who have not studied psychology, have not studied sociology, have not studied criminology, and then want to second-guess the outcome of a criminal investigation or dictate how law enforcement officers are supposed to do their job. It is my belief that whatever the truth is, these investigators should be commended for their efforts, and their findings should at least be considered for review.

In 1994 I made a trip to Britain. I was fortunate enough to travel all around London and made day trips to Bathe, South Hampton, Dover, and many other towns. While in London I visited the Greenwich Royal Observatory. The observatory was created in 1675, while it has moved and gone through many changes, it is still operational today. While I toured the facility, I was not only amazed at the history of the observatory, but at the equipment as well. Our tour guide was a very professional and experienced astronomer with a PhD. I found his talk fascinating, and then he elaborated on his belief that Earth is the only habitable planet in the universe. I was totally shocked. In 1992, astronomers had found the first exoplanet; he had to know this.

This discovery gave proof that planets do form outside our solar system—something I knew intuitively. This would lead to billions and billions of possibilities, but no; he firmly stuck to his hypothesis that the Earth is so unique, so special, that not only is there not life on other worlds, but there has not been, and there will not be. This man is a scientist who should be relying on physical observations and statistical probabilities. But his answer was no.

Period.

This is where our conundrum begins. This PhD of astronomy affirms there is no possibility of life elsewhere. He is a professor inferred to believe in the scientific method. A professor who believes in mathematics and statistics. A learned person who understands probability, and he just says, "No." It is this that we have to contend with. On one end of the spectrum, you have people who believe aliens are occupying the seats of government and are controlling our lives, and on the other end is the foundation of logic that contradicts its own probabilities. We are unlikely to be able to reason with either of these two extremes.

And it is in this realm the Roswell investigators must navigate.

I first met the famous **Stanton Friedman** in about 2007. I was fortunate enough to speak with him in Roswell at the annual convention. I introduced myself as law enforcement and former military, and we discussed the Roswell case a little, but mainly talked about the convention and some of the other speakers. The following morning, I was at the same hotel and saw him going into the restaurant, followed by a couple of men who were asking him questions on Majestic 12. I got in line behind them, and when he looked back, he excused himself from their conversation as if he had been waiting for me to arrive, and simply said to the waitress, "How about over there." He then just started a conversation with me, I don't remember what about, and again excused himself from his two inquisitors. We started following the waitress, and he whispered to me, "Get me away from these guys." We sat down at the table, and that is how I had breakfast with Stanton Friedman. He told me that one of the two men spent most of the previous day at Stanton's table basically arguing conspiracy theories with him. My presence saved him from a breakfast continuation of the same.

Stanton was a kind and interesting man. Even though authors Charles Berlitz and William Moore were the first to write a widely popular and distributed book on the event, titled *The Roswell Incident*, Friedman can be formally credited for the resurrection of the interest in the story. While the topic of something strange happening at Roswell publicly surfaced a couple of times prior to Friedman's work with Marcel, the tales were largely ignored. It was his persistence and dedication that brought Roswell into the light for all to see. I believe that his book *Crash at Corona*, with aviation science writer Don Berliner, provided a plausible explanation for the events in New Mexico in July 1947. Based on the documents Stanton and Don researched and the civilian and military personnel they interviewed, their hypothesis of an initial high-velocity impact area on the Foster Ranch and another site where the vehicle came to rest nearer to Corona, New Mexico, was conceivable. It made sense due to the little debris found at the Foster Ranch that a craft coming in at an angle with great speed would impact the ground and skip off, going airborne again until slowing velocity and gravity brought it back down. This would expectedly leave material behind at the initial impact site.

In his efforts to push his hypothesis, Stanton had a long running debate or "debates" with vocal debunker **Philip J. Klass**. He was a serious critic of Friedman. Not only did Klass debate the findings and methodology of other ufologists, but he also demanded a higher standard and burden of proof from those who would claim events were automatically extraterrestrial. While he was not liked in many circles, he nevertheless made a serious impact within the field of ufology.

Probably the most famous disagreement Klass and Friedman had was over the Majestic 12 (MJ-12) documents in 1984. The documents were obtained anonymously by ufologist Jamie Shandera when he received film negatives with pictures of the documents that were later reproduced. These were then disseminated by Shandera, Friedman and fellow author and ufologist William Moore. The MJ-12 documents were touted by these men as evidence to support the cover-up of the 1947 UFO crash and recovery in Roswell, reportedly orchestrated at the directions of then President Harry S. Truman. It outlines a series of twelve high-level government officials who were involved in coordinating the scheme and cover-up. The MJ-12 documents were later assessed as being fakes by many military document researchers and others, mainly due to inconsistencies in the verbiage and layout of the military memorandums themselves. The MJ-12 hypothesis was further exacerbated by the 1995 film *Alien Autopsy*. In the seventeen-minute black-and-white film, supposed military doctors conduct an autopsy on an alien cadaver recovered at the Roswell flying saucer crash site in 1947. Unfortunately, the film was later proved to be a fraud by its director. However, even testimony by the creator himself, Ray Santilli, will not dissuade some UFO researchers who continue to believe the government pressured the filmmakers into saying it was a fake to further the cover-up (Alien). Please feel free to research MJ-12 and the *Alien Autopsy* film further on your own, because I am not going any further down these rabbit holes...

To put it simply, Klass was extremely knowledgeable about all things UFO, and he was extremely skeptical of UFO reports. Tom Longden wrote in the Gannett Company's newspaper, *Des Moines Register*, that Klass said:

"'I've found, that roughly 97, 98 percent of the people who report seeing UFOs are fundamentally intelligent, honest people who have seen something—usually at night, in darkness —that is unfamiliar, that they cannot explain.' The rest, he said, were frauds."

Des Moines Register

Klass would routinely get into public and private debates/arguments with Friedman. In a September 12, 1991, article in the *Chicago Reader*, writer Cate Plys wrote that if Klass saw Friedman giving an interview, he would "shout things like, 'Can I buy some of your snake oil, Mr. Friedman?'" Needless to say, the two men's banter was entertaining to both sides of the argument, and like MJ-12, this facilitated more interest in Roswell, Friedman, and Klass.

One of the odd things about the UFO inquiry related to Roswell is that many of the key events of what Charles Berlitz and William Moore wrote about in their 1980 book, *The Roswell Incident*, was either directly or indirectly supported by the findings of the 1994 Air Force report. In their 1980 publication, Berlitz and Moore related their findings as (1) the weather balloon was a cover story, (2) that the debris was ultimately flown to Wright Field (Wright Patterson AFB, Dayton, Ohio), and (3) the material used for the staged photos in General Ramey's office was that of a weather balloon not the original material or that of what the Air Force says was MOGUL. And if the MJ-12 documents were a hoax (I say they were—yep, I said it...), they were most likely created in order to bolster the support for other accusations in the book. Or maybe to hoax the men; either way MJ-12 is a nope for me.

In 1980, when Berlitz and Moore contended the weather balloon explanation was a cover story, it was taken as an unsubstantiated, full-blown, put-on-your-foil-hats conspiracy theory. Yet Kevin Randle and Don Schmitt interviewed General

Thomas DuBose and quoted him in their 1991 book, *UFO Crash at Roswell*. DuBose was one of only a few people who possibly viewed the actual material brought from Roswell by Marcel, and one of only a few persons to personally view the balloon debris staged in Ramey's office. He was still alive up to February 1992 to tell the tale, and in a home-recorded video interview, he confirmed the conspiracy directly:

> *"... it was a cover story, the balloon part of it... is the story that it [sic] to be given to the press, and that is it, and—and anything else, forget it."*
>   Video of Brigadier General
>   Thomas Jefferson DuBose

This interview would have been one of the corroborative pieces of evidence that Berlitz and Moore needed to legitimize their hypothesis of what happened at Roswell. This too is what is so frustrating about the 1994 Air Force report—the complete disregard for a general's testimony. Included in the 1995 Air Force report identified as #6 Memo, with Attachments, is a paper titled "Synopsis of the Roswell Incident." In this, DuBose is reported saying:

> *"... officials at the Headquarters of the Eighth Air Force were directed to tell the press that the material was from a weather balloon radar target, and that the weather balloon explanation was a 'cover story' to divert the attention of the press."*
>   The Roswell Report –
>   Fact vs Fiction in the New Mexico Desert

Even though the Air Force men knew about General DuBose's involvement, and his name had come up in Professor Moore's interview referencing the "cover story," the Air Force does not reference General DuBose anywhere in their documentation or anywhere in their official summary or report. To completely ignore such a statement from one of the Air Force's own generals is one thing, but to completely remove or exclude pertinent and germane testimony is direct evidence of a further conspiracy or incompetence on the part of the Air Force in this matter. Not only is DuBose referenced in the Air Force's own attachments, but interviews with him are also easily found.

The Air Force investigators were well aware of DuBose. Ufologist, researcher, and author Kevin Randle has written extensively on DuBose and the fact that DuBose is on the record with several researchers and reporters saying he never actually saw the material brought from Roswell, just the staged balloon parts. In a July/August 1997 article of the *Skeptical Inquirer* titled "What Really Happened at Roswell," author Kal K. Korff accuses Maj. Jesse Marcel of a "bait and switch." Korff writes:

> *"Unfortunately for the pro-UFO Roswell advocates, the source of the claim that the wreckage in Ramey's office was replaced by that of a weather balloon is none other than, once again, Major Jesse Marcel."*
> Kal K. Korff

Based on DuBose's statements alone, I can conclude that I do not know what Marcel brought from Roswell; however, I do believe it was not the material in the disputed photos. I realize I am discounting Irving Newton's testimony that Marcel tried to convince him otherwise, but to me, the weather balloon cover-up is more consistent with the Air Force's behavior at the time. And it just makes more sense to me. All of this information was known to the 1994 Air Force report investigators, and either by higher orders, or by scheming investigative design, General DuBose was the victim of what we would today call Air Force cancel culture.

He does not exist.

During this highly convoluted conspiracy, Kevin Randall has evolved into one of the most pragmatic researchers into the 1947 events at Roswell. As a prolific writer of over eighty fiction and nonfiction books, he has explored every possible angle of the Roswell events. Like other researchers and writers on the topic, he has been a victim of personal assassination by those in the field with differing opinions, has had his methods questioned, and his outcomes scrutinized. But this is all part of the process when you are dealing with an investigation.

Rarely are they cut and dry.

I have been a professional law enforcement officer for thirty plus years. I have worked in local law enforcement as a patrol officer, a mental health investigator, an academy instructor, a major crimes detective, an underwater evidence recovery specialist, as a patrol sergeant and a lieutenant. In the military I was assigned as a master-at-arms in the US Navy (Navy military police/security) and as a firearms instructor in the Security Forces (formerly known as security police) of the Air Force. There is not a report I have written, not a form I have filled out, not an investigation I have led, that someone/anyone could come review and say I should have done this, or they would have done that. The real problem is if the process of the gathered information lies so far out of the accepted practice, so far away from the industry standard, to be deemed not reliable. It is part of the process—no researcher or investigator should be afraid of peer review. Peer review helps refine your process, adjust your hypothesis, and apply lessons learned for your future.

Kevin Randle and Don Schmitt collaborated on two popular books about Roswell: *UFO Crash at Roswell* in 1991, and *The Truth About the UFO Crash at Roswell* in 1994. In the years after, criticism of the works and differing opinions of the outcomes seemed to force the two men apart. Allegations of improper investigative process, or lack thereof, and accusations of outright dishonesty were tossed about by their detractors like careless hand grenades—the shrapnel of which not only damaged the two men, but others with whom they were affiliated.

Schmitt was specifically attacked on his credentials and methods. Probably the most serious public debate surrounded Philip Klass's 1995 *Skeptics UFO Newsletter* article titled "Roswell Crashed-Saucer Researcher Randle Admits he was Taken in by Co-Author Schmitt's Tall Tales." Klass pulled no punches about Schmitt's lack of truthfulness about his academic and employment history. His accusation and the revelation of this to the UFO community hit the credibility of the Roswell investigation hard.

Later, additional disparagers spoke of Randle confusing his research work with his fictional novels—an absurd allegation to those who know Randle and his passion for credibility. While Randle and others were damaged by the controversy, Randle has always remained a conscientious, believable, and trustworthy researcher. In the case of Frankie Rowe, his stoicism in defense of her story is noteworthy.

Frankie came under fire by debunkers after she had relayed a story she said was told by her father, Dan Dwyer, a Roswell fireman. Frankie said when she was about twelve years old, her father told her he had responded to a call outside the city and had come upon a wrecked spacecraft with a living alien. She further explained that some of the men brought back material from the craft, later referred to by investigators as memory metal. Hearing this story, debunkers went to work and could find no supportive evidence of Frankie's claims and furthermore depended on the testimony of other retired firemen (none from 1947) that they did not respond to calls outside the city—this is the proof the debunkers relied on. Which was later proven to be untrue.

Either way, Frankie's story is just another that can neither be supported by evidence nor debunked by proven fabrications. The criticisms of Frankie's story continue to this day. Her tale is merely left up to the reader to decide whether you believe her or not.

Most of these attacks on Roswell and the credibility of the investigations conducted are fueled from every direction and essentially has forced a pressing of the "reset button" of the Roswell events. The Randle-Schmitt schism actually helped to create a better foundation for the Roswell facts. It helped increase the credibility of the information gathered about the event and had new researchers more closely qualifying their witnesses, evaluating their evidence, and relying less on speculation—the false narratives became much more discoverable.

Since the Klass article and others, Don Schmitt has endeavored to defend his reputation and repair his credibility. We must all realize these accusations were over twenty-five years ago, and whatever his critics said he was then, he is a different man today, as are most of you now reading this text. There is one thing I know to be true, if you do everything correctly, every time, you learn nothing. I believe over the last two decades Don Schmitt has learned much. Each of us learn best from our mistakes if we learn from anything at all. And as long as we are not afraid of making mistakes, we will continue to benefit from the course.

Since the 1995 article Don has written multiple books with Tom Carey, *Witness to Roswell, Cover-Up at Roswell, Roswell the Ultimate Cold Case,* and others. He has been on hundreds of interviews, TV, and radio shows, was a consultant for *Roswell* the TV series and *Unsolved Mysteries.* Don and Tom organized archaeological digs at the reported crash site on the Foster Ranch, and he has spoken hundreds of times at various public and private events. As any experienced person knows, the more exposure you have, the more darkened corners you search, the more likely you are to make mistakes. The more likely assassins will get you in their sights. Oddly, people will more often point out your deficiencies than tout your successes.

I commend Don not only for owning his misjudgments but for the huge contributions he and Tom Carey have made to investigating Roswell and to the UFO community in general. The thousands of hours they have dedicated to research and the thousands of dollars they have spent traveling to meet with witnesses and other investigators is a testament to their dedication of truth seeking. We all must remember Stanton Friedman's rules of debunking listed in a June 2002 *MUFON UFO Journal* article titled "Pseudoscience of Anti-ufology." Especially rule number three.

1. Don't bother me with the facts; my mind is made up
2. What the public and media don't know, don't tell them
3. If you can't attack the data, attack the people; it's easier
4. Do your research by proclamation, rather than investigation

There is no doubt that cynical debunkers can use these very rules against a uniformed or unprepared investigator, but know if you delve off into the realm of the UFO phenomena, you will likely face single-focused assassins. Also known in today's vernacular as "haters.", and "haters" gonna hate...

An example of someone else of UFO prominence who was also accused of deceptions (actually there have been many, and I am picking the ones I feel are most notable and influenced the Roswell investigation) would be former CIA intelligence officer, consultant, Deputy Assistant Secretary of Defense for Operational Test and Evaluation, editor, and author Karl T. Pflock. For a while, Pflock suffered a similar fate to Don Schmitt. He described himself as a "hopeful agnostic" (and so do I) and went on to write most notably *Roswell: Inconvenient Facts and the Will to Believe.* This was a hard-hitting research endeavor by Pflock to flush out the truth about the purported 1947 recovery of a crashed flying saucer and aliens in the New Mexico Desert. He believed that his research approach, relying primarily on declassified government documents and select reported Roswell witnesses, brought him to the truth. His conclusion was simple:

> *"This body of testimony and evidence establishes beyond a reasonable doubt that alien voyagers were not shipwrecked here over a half century ago."*
> Karl Pflock

Given Pflock's credentials, education, and experience, one would think his apparent unbiased research and impartial opinion would leave little to debate. However, this is not the case in the UFO world. And that was not the case with his book either. Pflock did provide his own subjective opinions and went on a personal attack of the pro-Roswell believers:

> *"The advocates of the crashed saucer tale, wittingly or not, simply shovel everything that seems to support their views into the box labeled 'Evidence' and say, 'See?' Look at all this stuff. We must be right. Never mind the contradictions. Never mind the lack of independent supporting fact. Never mind the blatant absurdities."*
> Roswell: Inconvenient Facts and the Will to Believe

Unfortunately, when you decide the avenue of personal attack as opposed to narrowing down and refuting specific facts, you can expect reprisals. By saying this, he opened the door to any Roswell researcher who may be of the opinion that there is the possibility that the US government concealed their knowledge of what actually happened in the Roswell affair. It didn't take long before Pflock was dodging critical reviews of his work and ducking potshots at his credibility. And like Don Schmitt before him, he found himself having to defend his deceptions after lying about his name to the authors of the book *Mute Evidence: The Cattle Mutilations Mystery—Solved!* Kevin Randle effectively addresses the controversy in his blog *A Different Perspective*. In a 2015 article titled "Kurt Peters, Karl Pflock and Don Schmitt" Randle skillfully addresses lie comparisons by concluding:

> *"In the world of Ufology the side you take up is usually the one that falls under your own belief structure. Sometimes it has less to do with evidence and more to do with what you wish to believe."*
> Kevin Randle

Randle's statement is truer than you think. When I initially started seriously researching Roswell, I was of the mindset of a criminal investigator searching for "proof beyond a reasonable doubt." It is that burden of proof that a prosecutor must establish for a guilty verdict in a criminal case. I had briefly spoken with Don Schmitt about the burden of proof at an annual Roswell convention around 2008. Don undoubtedly, unwaveringly confirmed he absolutely believes, beyond a reasonable doubt, the US government recovered a crashed flying saucer and four beings. And at that time, he indicated that if the Roswell Incident were a criminal case, a grand jury would indict. And Don's assertion is supported by many noteworthy opinions. Solomon Wachtler, former Chief Judge of the New York Court of Appeals, was quoted in a 1985 New York Daily News' interview with Marcia Kramer and Frank Lombardi that:

"… district attorneys now have so much influence on grand juries that 'by and large' they could get them to 'indict a ham sandwich.'"

Judge Solomon Wachtler

At that time and today, I *do believe* there is a reasonable doubt that the US government recovered a crashed flying saucer and four beings from another planet and have secluded them at a secret location. However, based on the mere volume of the sworn testimony of the professed witnesses interviewed, and strange circumstances that surround the Roswell events, I believe it would be found to be true in a civil proceeding. As the burden of proof is not "beyond a reasonable doubt," but based on a "preponderance of the evidence." And this is a topic that Tom Carey and Don Schmitt address in their 2020 book *Roswell: The Ultimate Cold Case.*

With the aforementioned researchers and many others whom I did not have time to address in this book, the Roswell Incident captured the imaginations of millions of people from countries all around the world. It is doubtful that the topic would be as profound today without the contributions of Josef Allen Hynek, PhD of astrophysics. Hynek has been portrayed as the official UFO hunter for the US government in books, television programs and movies. While his character is often fictionalized surrounded by alien-related circumstances, his real-world contributions to the UFO phenomena are numerous.

Hynek was initially involved with UFOs as a consultant for the United States Air Force Project Sign. His main job was to determine, based on the UFO report, if the object was a known celestial object or not. He was, in effect, hired as the government's debunker. However, over the years Hynek reviewed enough reports and saw enough examples that in 1953 he wrote a report titled "Unusual Aerial Phenomena" (UAP) for the *Journal of the Optical Society of America.* Oddly enough, years later, the government would begin to refer to UFOs as UAPs, unidentified aerial phenomena. In the article, Hynek defends his and others' observation of lights in the night skies as worthy of scientific attention. Hynek's interest was piqued not only from the volume of UFO reports, but from who was making them. He felt people representing professional occupations such as police officers and pilots, people who are trained to make observations, were particularly intriguing.

Hynek went into both Project Sign and later Project Grudge as a hard-core skeptic. He has been quoted as saying that he felt the subject of UFOs was ridiculous. However, one of the things that changed his mind about UFOs was the Air Force's insistence on naturally explaining every reported event away, and contending with their adverse attitude toward spending any effort on the subject. The findings seemed unimportant and bothersome.

Much the way the 1994 Air Force investigation was conducted...

Therefore, Hynek's position ultimately legitimized the extraterrestrial possibilities.

OF THE POSSIBILITIES

THE CRASH AND THE DRAKE EQUATION

THERE ARE MANY POSSIBILITIES THAT LIFE HAS EVOLVED ON other planets. Actually, according to Harvard University's Harlow Shapley, there are too many possibilities for the human brain to comprehend. He estimated the number to be one hundred thousand million billion stars capable through radiation to maintain photochemical reactions suitable for plant and animal life (Shapley). Thus, he deduced there are at least one hundred million suitable planetary systems. Don't try to comprehend it, our brains cannot grasp the size or complexity. Nor can we grasp the vastness of space and the distances between solar systems, not to mention the distance between galaxies within the observable universe. But distance is only part of the problem; the other problem is time. While life may have formed on another planetary body, it may have formed two billion years ago and since died out. Even if they developed into a complex society with advanced space travel and communication modes we can't even imagine, our timeline may not be aligned with any of them. And even if it did, how then do you conquer the vastness of space and the time it takes whatever communication carrier they use to make it to Earth. And how would we know what to look for, or which way to look?

Anyone who has imagined such things, who has looked to the sky and wondered, who has researched the possibilities is steered toward American astronomer and astrophysicist Frank Drake. According to the SETI Institute, Dr. Drake created a rudimentary formula to estimate the number of societies in the Milky Way Galaxy that may have or had developed into a culture advanced enough to transmit using radio waves. For those of you who do not already know, the Drake equation is:

$$N = R * f_p * n_e * f_l * f_i * f_c * L$$

- N = Number of civilizations whose electromagnetic emissions are detectable
- R = Rate of star creation suitable for life
- f_p = Fraction of stars that have planets
- n_e = Number of habitable planets (Earth-like)
- f_l = Fraction of planets where life evolves
- f_i = Fraction of planets with intelligent life
- f_c = Fraction of planets capable of interstellar communication
- L = Lifespan of the civilization

In doing such a calculation in 1961, science at that time had yet to detect planetary bodies outside our own solar system—the men were merely speculating. It wasn't until 1992 that astronomers Aleksander Wolszczan and Dale Frail discovered evidence of the first exoplanet (Winn). So, in an observable universe of containing about a billion trillion stars and using 2019 numbers of just over 4,000 exoplanets with 55 in the "Goldilocks Zone," that would leave us with about 50 billion habitable planets in the Milky Way alone. There are over 100 billion galaxies out there...

Then comes the 1997 Air Force's rebuttal to all the criticism generated from their original report, *The Roswell Incident* –

Fact vs Fiction in the New Mexico Desert. This one titled *The Roswell Report – Case Closed.* Compiled and written by Captain James McAndrew, the same James McAndrew who co-authored *The Roswell Incident* as a lieutenant. And like before, the Air Force concentrated on plausible explanations instead of addressing obvious documented inconsistencies within credible witness accounts. The Air Force report concentrated on the already impeached statements of Jim Ragsdale, Vern Maltais, Gerald Anderson (that I didn't even bother to cover in depth), and Glenn Dennis. Yet it gave absolutely no mention of consideration to the sworn statement of eyewitness General Thomas DuBose, *again*; a glaring omission in my opinion.

In the Air Force's ultimate conclusion, they summarize their position well in a single paragraph:

> *"When critically examined, the claim that the US Army Air forces recovered a flying saucer in [sic] alien crew in 1947, were found to be a complication of many variable events. For the most part, the descriptions collected by UFO theorists were of actual operations and tests carried out by the US Air Force in the 1950s."*
> *The Roswell Report* 1997

It is apparent that officials of the United States Air Force have and will continue to maintain there is no proof of extraterrestrial visitation to Earth. There is no evidence of spaceships from other planets visiting our planet. And there was no celestial spacecraft or aliens recovered in the New Mexico desert. Thus the Air Force simply relies on the Fermi paradox: If there are so many possibilities of life on other planet such as the Drake equation suggests, where are all the aliens? The problem with that logic is it doesn't follow. Just because we have not observed something does not mean it does not exist. There are so many variables to explain the absence of extraterrestrial contact such as evolutionary (their timeline does not match our own), sociological (they may be isolationists, only settled in one part of the galaxy, or not even live on planets), or economic (have a lack of resources for deep space travel). The point is, the absence of evidence does not equate to evidence of absence. I will say it again:

The absence of evidence does not equate to the evidence of absence.

As far as the extraterrestrial question, at this point the only thing that will satisfy most of the US population is full and total disclosure—the Air Force has lied to us so many times that I say we can no longer trust their explanations in the matter of UFOs/UAPs or whatever other three-letter abbreviation you choose. But any explanation put forward needs to be reviewed by a credible third party and must be fact checked. At this point, anything less than the Air Force rolling out the spaceship and alien bodies will be trivial.

As I stated in the beginning of this book, the intent here is to identify lessons learned from our (everyone involved) mistakes, and we made plenty. But I can say, the information I have collected, the interviews I have conducted, and the overall circumstances reported by Roswell researchers of the Roswell Incident leave gaping questions of the overall consistency and strength of the investigation as a whole. If a single clearinghouse were to impeach discredited witness accounts, intentional hoaxes, and evidentiary falsehoods, leaving only the depositions of credible witnesses, the overall foundation and validity of the event would change.

Cornell Law School defines that the "preponderance of the evidence" is met when:

"... the party with the burden (of proof) *convinces the fact*

finder that there is a greater than 50% chance that the claim is true."

In the case of the Roswell Incident, the "fact finder(s)" is those persons of the United States public that know the circumstances described by the witnesses of the event and can make an informed determination—a consensus of the people. If the Roswell Incident was simply a civil disagreement between parties, one of which (the petitioner—the Roswell investigators) had dozens of credible citizens and military personnel come forward with information that supports their assertion of a crashed spaceship, and the other (the respondent—the Air Force) brought only hand-selected and coached persons forward, excluded individuals whose testimony they disagreed with yet was germane to the situation, and was known to repeatedly be deceitful about the facts of the investigation, this case would receive a quick and simple ruling on the matter. The findings would conclude: **In 1947, an alien craft was recovered in the New Mexico desert.**

On the other hand, if the Roswell case were brought before a criminal court with its burden of proof being "beyond a reasonable doubt," this case would receive a quick and simple ruling on the matter. The findings would conclude: **A mistrial due to the government's [Air Force's] coaching of witnesses and its perceived violations of [evidentiary] discovery.**

But—the facts remain. We do not have a court to rule over these circumstances; therefore until the military releases the entire case file on Roswell or, better yet, releases information they have an extraterrestrial vehicle and aliens in their possession, the circumstances of the Roswell Incident will languish in the ether, ripe for continued debate and further ridicule.

Oddly, the only people who can ever be proved to be wrong

in this matter are the debunkers. And they don't seem to mind. Most of them, like most of the rest of us, would love to have the knowledge of an alien visitation, but most just don't believe it was Roswell. And they are willing to remain stoic on the matter, firmly denying any possibilities of an extraterrestrial event.

Despite further cynicism, we do know that (1) there was a conspiracy to conceal the "event," (2) there was disinformation intentionally spread by the government to confuse the facts of the "event," (3) the government remained dishonest in their disclosure of the "event," and (4) the government suppressed and/or eliminated witness information that would potentially damage their explanation of MOGUL. If anyone argues these facts, they have not considered the government's position or learned from their mistakes.

Many debunkers try to use Roswell as the litmus test for their argument against the possibility that aliens traveled through space and visited the Earth. These debunkers in one sentence will vehemently refute the Drake equation while religiously reciting the Fermi paradox. To me, these sets of topics are two completely different claims. Two completely different philosophies that the believer or disbeliever has entrenched themselves in. To prove this to be incorrect, you would need to bring forward the hundreds of credible people who claim visitations or alien abduction experiences outside of Roswell. You would need to discredit each of the stories of experiencers such as Travis Walton, Betty and Barney Hill, and many others as flights of fancy or outright hoaxes. You would need to explain away all the people who have never been diagnosed with a mental illness or been known to suffer from delusions or hallucinations.

I attended one of Jesse Marcel Jr.'s last presentations at the International UFO Museum and Research Center in Roswell. In typical Jesse Jr. fashion, he was introspective, engaging, and full of possibilities. The events he experienced when he was a kid, the material his father brought to their home and he examined, and the Roswell UFO and alien fervor manifested from his father's passion to tell the truth had seemed to spur something within him. Jesse Marcel Jr. believed more than most in the potential of life on faraway planets. That his belief of alien life on another world did not threaten the idea of God and the concept of heaven in the afterlife. He did not believe these two ideas were exclusive of one another. He always remained hopeful.

I am on the side of Jesse Jr.—I don't know exactly what happened out in the desert. But I am one who believes in the possibilities.

I will be keeping my fingers crossed.

WORKS CITED

Army Air Forces. (n.d.). US Army. Retrieved June 12, 2021, https://www.army.mil/aviation/airforces/index.html

Biography of Wernher Von Braun. (n.d.). NASA.gov, Retrieved April 17, 2021, https://www.nasa.gov/centers/marshall/history/vonbraun/bio.html

Blanchard, R. (2019, February 12) *Sobering Stats: 15,000 U.S. Airmen Killed in Training in WW II.* Real Clear History. https://www.realclearhistory.com/articles/2019/02/12/staggering_statistics_15000_us_airmen_killed_in_training_in_ww_ii_412.html

Cherry, K. (2020). *False Memories and How They Are Formed.* Verywell Mind. https://www.verywellmind.com/how-do-false-memories-form-2795349

Cornel Law School. (n.d.) Preponderence of the Evidence. *Legal Information Institute.* Retrieved June 15, 2021, https://www.law.cornell.edu/wex/preponderance_of_the_evidence

Correll, J.T. (2020). Hitler's Buzz Bombs. Air Force Magazine. https://www.airforcemag.com/article/hitlers-buzz-bombs/

General William H. Blanchard. (n.d.). US Air Force. Retrieved May 12, 2021, https://www.af.mil/About-Us/Biographies/Display/Article/107667/general-william-h-blanchard/

Gross, P. (2017, May 20). *Roswell 1947 - Documents on the Witnesses: Charle Forgus.* UFOs at Close Sight. https://ufologie.patrickgross.org/rw/w/charlesforgus.htm

Hynek, J.A. (1953). Unusual Aerial Phenomena. *Journal of the Optical Society of America,* vol. 43, Issue 4, pp. 311-314. https://www.osapublishing.org/josa/viewmedia.cfm?uri=josa-43-4-311&seq=0&html=true

In Memory of Sheriff George Wilcox: The Human Tragedy of Roswell. (2016, October 7). The Cosmic Switchboard. Retrived June 22, 2021, https://www.thecosmicswitchboard.com/2016/10/07/george-wilcox-human-tragedy-roswell/

Insights on Roswell. (1996, October 6). VJ Enterprises. Retrieved June 12, 2021, http://www.v-j-enterprises.com/jbond.html

International Socialist Review, Vol.20 No.2, Spring 1959, pp.61-62.

Krazney, Z. (2016, August). *What Were the Mysterious "Foo Fighters" Sighted by WWII Night Flyers?* Air & Space Magazine. https://www.airspacemag.com/history-of-flight/what-were-mysterious-foo-fighters-sighted-ww2-night-flyers-180959847/

Launching a Vision. (n.d.) Kennedy Biographies. NASA.gov. Retrieved April 17, 2021, https://www.nasa.gov/centers/kennedy/about/biographies/debus.html

Lewis D. (2016, November 16). *Why the U.S. Government Brought Nazi Scientists to America After World War II.* Smithsonian Magazine. https://www.smithsonianmag.com/smart-news/why-us-government-brought-nazi-scientists-america-after-world-war-ii-180961110/

Liljegren, A. (n.d.). *Project 1946: The Ghost Rocket Documents Released by the Swedish Defence Staff.* Archieves for UFO Research. http://www.ignaciodarnaude.com/avistamientos_ovnis/Liljegren,Ghost%20Rockets%201946,Sweden,FS-R86V32N1.pdf

Nuremberg Trials. (n.d.) United States Holicost Memorial Museum. Retrieved June 15, 2021, https://encyclopedia.ushmm.org/content/en/article/the-nuremberg-trials

Operation Crossroads. (2014, July 1). Atomic Heritage Foundation. Retrieved June 2, 2021, https://www.atomicheritage.org/history/operation-crossroads

Payne Jennings (n.d.). Army Air Corps Museum. Retrieved January 12, 2021, https://www.armyaircorpsmuseum.org/missing-in-action/jennings-payne-mia-90751.cfm

Pflock, K. (2001). *Roswell - Inconveniet Facts and the Will to Believe.* Prometheus Books, (pp. 34, 120, 171-172).

Philip J. Corso's Department of the Army Form 66, Officer Qualification Record. (1997, August 4). The Computer UFO

Network. Retrieved June 12, 2021, https://www.cufon.org/cufon/corso_da66.htm

Pierce, Marlyn R., (2013), *Earning Their Wings: Accidents and Fatalities in the United States Army Air Forces During Flight Training in World War Two*. Doctoral dissertation, Kansas State University. pg. XV. https://core.ac.uk/download/pdf/18529342.pdf

Printy, T. (1999). The Joker and the Spaceship. Astronomy UFO. http://www.astronomyufo.com/UFO/Rickett.htm

Project Sign. (n.d.). Wikia.org. Retrieved June 2, 2021, https://military.wikia.org/wiki/Project_Sign

Randle, K. (2017, July 21). *Alleged Roswell Witness Update*. A Different Perspective. http://kevinrandle.blogspot.com/2017/07/alleged-roswell-witness-update.html

Randle, K. (2007, May 12). *The DuBose Affidavit*. A Different Perspective. http://kevinrandle.blogspot.com/2007/05/DuBose-affidavit.html

Saxe, L. (2011, December 22). *Lies, lies, lies*. Management Issues. https://www.management-issues.com/opinion/6370/lies-lies-lies/

Schmitt, D. (Director). (1997). UFO Crash at Roswell: Audio Documentary. Baraka Foundation.

Shalett, S. (1949, April 30). *What You Can Believe About Flying Saucers*. Project 1947. http://www.project1947.com/fig/satevepost_43049.htm

Shapley, Harlow. *Of Stars and Men*. Beacon Press, 1958

Smithsonian National Air and Space Museum. (April 22, 2011). *Ask an Expert: The Roswell Incident.* YouTube. https://www.youtube.com/watch?v=foJWblpzEjA&t=477s

The American Legion. (2015, November 10). *World War II pilot sculpts life size monument to recognize fallen airmen.* https://www.legion.org/stories/community-memorials-monuments/world-war-ii-pilot-sculpts-lifesize-monument-recognize-fallen

The Children Who Bore Witness to Roswell: Their Tragic Stories Finally Revealed. (n.d.) UFO Explorations. Retrieved April 3, 2021, https://www.ufoexplorations.com/children-who-bore-witness-roswell

Terry, Vaught, and Hays. *The Ultimate Trail Notebook: Family Law – Witness Preparation.* State Bar of Texas, 2000.

United States Air Force. (1995). *The Roswell Report: Fact vs. Fiction in the New Mexico Desert.* https://media.defense.gov/2010/Dec/01/2001329893/-1/-1/0/roswell-2.pdf

Weaver, Richard. *Backstory: Roswell Exclusive Untold Disclosures About the 1994 Air Force Roswell Report Told by the Man Who Lead the Inquiry.* Self-Published, 2020.

Wikipedia Contributors. "Alien Autopsy." *Wikipedia.* Wikimedia Foundation, 27 September 2019, https://en.wikipedia.org/w/index.php?title=Alien_autopsy&action=history. Accessed 3 July 2021.

Wikipedia Contributors. *"ASM-A-1 Tarzon."* Wikipedia. Wikimedia Foundation, 31 July 2011, https://en.wikipedia.org/wiki/ASM-A-1_Tarzon. Accessed 23 June 2021.

Wikipedia Contributors. *International Military Tribunal for the Far East.* Wikipedia. Wikimedia Foundation, 1 October 2004, https://en.wikipedia.org/wiki/International_Military_Tribunal_for_the_Far_East. Accessed 12 April 2021.

Winn, J.N. (2019, November 12) Who Really Discovered the First Exoplanet? *Scientific American.* https://blogs.scientificamerican.com/observations/who-really-discovered-the-first-exoplanet/

World Population Review. (n.d.). *World War II Casualties by Country. The National World War II Museum.* Retrieved June 8, 2021, https://worldpopulationreview.com/country-rankings/world-war-two-casualties-by-country

Zaragoza, M. S., & Lane, S. M. (1994). Source misattributions and the suggestibility of eyewitness memory. *Journal of Experimental Psychology: Learning, Memory, and Cognition,* 20(4), 934-945.

Writer, researcher, and career law enforcement officer, Greg Lawson, has authored five books on policing and investigating the paranormal. He is a police academy instructor and an international lecturer on the topics of paranormal perceptions. He lives in Central Texas with his wife Lynn, his dog Sockie and cats Minq, Tiggadeedo, Teetah Jamez, and Frank.

His work can be found at: www.theparanormaldetective.com

* 9 7 8 1 9 5 4 5 2 8 1 6 1 *